MIDWEST EDITION

Common Birds
of North America

AN EXPANDED GUIDEBOOK

James D. Wilson

D0916202

Willow Creek®
P R E S S

WEST BEND LIBRARY

MAP KEY

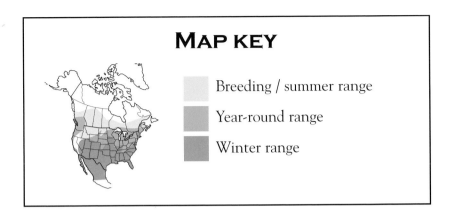

Breeding / summer range

Year-round range

Winter range

© 2001 James D. Wilson
Text and illustrations by James D. Wilson

Published by Willow Creek Press, P.O. Box 147, Minocqua, Wisconsin 54548

All rights reserved. No part of this book may be reproduced or transmitted in any form by any means, electronic or mechanical, including photocopying, recording, or by any information storage and retrieval system, without written permission from the Publisher.

Design by Patricia Bickner Linder
Edited by Andrea Donner

For information on other Willow Creek Press titles, call 1-800-850-9453

Library of Congress Cataloging-in-Publication Data
    Wilson, James D., 1943-
      Common birds of North America : an expanded guidebook / by James D.
    Wilson.--Midwest edition
        p. cm.
      ISBN 1-57223-301-X (softcover : alk. paper)
    1. Birds--Middle West--Identification. I. Title.
      QL683.M55 W56 2001
      598'.07'23478--dc21
                                                2001003684

Printed in Canada

598.072
W69

To Marsha, Christopher, and Corey

CONTENTS

INTRODUCTION

irds are our most conspicuous wildlife. They are active; many are brightly-colored with beautiful voices; and they are right out there for us to see, enjoy, and learn about — on fence wires, in treetops, over our heads, on our lawns, and as close as our bird feeders. It is quite natural that there is such interest in them. Most bird enthusiasts are not avid chasers of unusual bird species. They simply want to know the identity and something about the birds that they see around their homes, flitting outside their office windows, or flying overhead as they are stopped at a traffic light. Throughout my 24 years as a professional ornithologist with the Missouri Department of Conservation, people have contacted me regularly with their questions and observations about the common birds they see on a regular basis. It is people like these for whom this book is written.

This book addresses most questions about Midwestern birds by focusing on only the 90 most common species. By not including the birds that are less likely to be seen, the text can cover in detail the birds that are included, helping with identification and informing the reader about the particulars of the birds' biology. These 90 species represent at least 98 percent of the birds that a Midwesterner is likely to see. Though a few birds in this book may be less known, all are common enough that a person can become familiar with them with little effort. The key to seeing these birds is to watch birds in all seasons and to be aware of them wherever you are — at home, on walks through the park, and on drives through the countryside.

Each species is presented with a color illustration and an associated narrative. Most of the illustrations are simple portraits showing birds behaving as expected and in habitat typical for that species. These life-like portrayals are meant to impart identification cues, in addition to color and shape. They are also intended to inform visually about that bird's life history as they sometimes show nests, eggs, foods, and feeding behavior. Birds usually seen in the sky are shown from below. Those that perch in trees, bushes, or on the ground, are depicted with an example of the cover in which they might be found.

The narratives accompanying each illustration begin with a description of the species' physical characteristics, including those sexual and seasonal variations that are not depicted in the illustrations. They proceed to describe the bird's sound, habitat, feeding behavior, winter and summer ranges, and the dates of migration. For those that nest in the Midwest, the narratives conclude with a discussion of courtship behavior, nest location, color and number of eggs, and the length of time required for incubation and rearing. In some cases, human relationships to the featured bird are mentioned, such as methods of feeding, placement of nest boxes, or those that have been selected as State Birds.

For the purposes of this book, the Midwest is Illinois, Indiana, Iowa, Missouri, Wisconsin, Michigan, Minnesota, Ohio, Kentucky, Kansas, Nebraska, North and South Dakota, and adjacent provinces of Canada. Some of the birds featured are more common in certain portions of the region than others. A few, though numerous in certain locales, were not included if absent from the majority of the region. However, despite the large size of this geographical area, most of the birds featured are common throughout.

The arrangement of the birds in this book is standard with a few exceptions. It is based on a professional classification scheme that places closely related species together. Other bird literature is likely to cover them in the same sequence. Though this arrangement may seem confusing at first, it should be easy to find a bird of interest, given the relatively few birds covered in this book. A hint to success is to realize that the first 36 species include such diverse groups as waterfowl, large birds of prey, hummingbirds, and woodpeckers. The last 54 species are classified as songbirds or perching birds, beginning with the aerial insectivores and ending with those that have heavier bills for cracking seed coats. Two exceptions to this arrangement are the American Crow and American Tree Sparrow, which are songbirds placed in the first one-third of the book as part of compositions.

I had great fun painting these birds in the postures and habitats in which I have seen them on hundreds of occasions. It is hoped that they occasionally illicit an "Aha, that's just the way I saw it" response when you compare a sighting to my portrayal. With little effort, all of these birds can be seen and enjoyed. Birds are a diverse group, composed of truly unique and fascinating species. The bird facts that I have presented will, hopefully, help you to appreciate your feathered neighbors all the more.

Hints for Enjoying Birds

o get the most out of this book, be attentive to the birds wherever you are. Even when visual identification is not conclusive, many of the birds in this book can be identified from their behavior, the habitat where you see them, or by season of the year. Some, however, may require careful examination. Binoculars help in seeing details; use them to look for certain features before turning to the book as the bird may not remain in view for long. In addition to color, remember whether the bird has an eye-line, wing-bars, or a plain or streaked breast. Light spots on the tail characterize certain warblers, and leg and bill color can be useful in clarifying which sparrow or warbler has been seen.

Although some species of birds can be seen nearly everywhere, many are only associated with a particular kind of habitat. For example, Brown Thrashers live in brushy thickets, Eastern Meadowlarks reside in grassland, and Scarlet Tanagers are associated with the woods. Therefore, to see the variety presented in this book, be aware of birds when in a variety of places. Likewise, habitat can be an identification cue. A small blue bird in a forest edge would more likely be an Indigo Bunting than an Eastern Bluebird. Similarly, season of the year can provide a clue to identification. American Tree Sparrows, for example, are not expected in the Midwest in summer, so if a bird resembling one is seen in July, it is probably the similar-appearing Chipping Sparrow. A large part of successful bird identification is realizing what to expect, when and where.

Although we regularly hear birds sing and call, relatively few people are able to identify them by voice. Users of this book are encouraged to try to see the bird that is vocalizing so as to make a connection between the song that is described and the singer's actual identity. When auditory and visual identification concur, the learning of songs can begin to take place. Once tuned in to identifying birds by their voices, a new level of enjoyment can be achieved.

People who invite birds to their yards with feeders and nest boxes have an advantage in getting to know them. Sunflower seed, either in the shell or hulled, is most effective in attracting a diversity of delightful seed-eaters, including cardinals, chickadees, nuthatches, woodpeckers, and various finches. Juncos and sparrows that feed on the ground favor white-proso millet. Niger, or "thistle seed," though expensive, can be targeted to finches by using tubular, hanging feeders. Suet, or fat trimmings, attracts clinging birds such as woodpeckers, chickadees, and nuthatches; it can be provided for the birds in a mesh bag hung on a tree limb.

Most people provide bird feeding stations only in winter, when birds seem especially willing to accept hand-outs. Summertime feeding is becoming increasingly popular, however, because of the variety of birds that are visiting at that season, many in their brightest plumage of the year. Summer customers might include such brilliant seed-eaters as Indigo Buntings, Rose-breasted Grosbeaks, and American Goldfinches. The warm period of the year is also the time to invite hummingbirds and orioles with special feeders filled with a "nectar." Early spring is the time to put up nest boxes for the dozen or more species in this book that might use them. People who put up houses or search out nests are most likely to see the eggs, young, and the parental behaviors described in this book.

If your interest in birds extends beyond those covered in this book, there are numerous field guides on the market that address the identification of thousands of birds in all color phases and in all regions of the country and world. But realize that these primarily cover details relating to identification. There are few books, other than this one, that provide life history plus identification details on an extensive list of common birds within a particular region of the country.

ATTRACTING BIRDS TO FEEDERS

SPECIES	FAVORITE FOODS	NOTES
Mourning Dove	Cracked corn, Millet	Feeds on ground
Woodpeckers	Suet, Sunflower	Can cling to feed
Blue Jay	Sunflower, Corn	Avoids swinging feeders
Tufted Titmouse	Whole sunflower	Hanging feeder
Chickadee	Hulled sunflower	Can cling to feed
Nuthatch	Sunflower, Peanut butter	Latter smeared on bark
Starling	Suet, Table scraps	Feeds in flocks
Eastern Towhee	Sunflower, Millet	Summering bird
White-crowned Sparrow	Hulled sunflower, Peanut hearts	Feeds on ground
White-throated Sparrow	Hulled Sunflower, Millet	Feeds on ground
Dark-eyed Junco	Millet	Feeds on ground
Northern Cardinal	Sunflower, Safflower	Feeds from a perch
Rose-breasted Grosbeak	Sunflower	Summering bird
Indigo Bunting	Millet	Summering bird
Purple/House Finch	Niger seed, Sunflower	Feeds in flocks
Goldfinch/Siskin	Niger seed, Millet, Sunflower	Feeders with small perches
House Sparrow	Bread crumbs, Millet	Feeds in flocks
Hummingbird/Oriole	Nectar (1 part sugar to 4 water)	Specific feeder styles
Mockingbird/Catbird	Jelly, Cut-up fruit	Placed on board, Summer

IDENTIFICATION TIPS

► large, long-bodied, low-swimming

► stout, straight bill, evenly-tapered

► in summer, black and white checkered back and broken white collar

► in flight, the wingbeats are fast, uninterrupted by gliding; the head is carried lower than the body

COMMON LOON

Gavia immer

People in the lakes regions of Minnesota, Wisconsin, and Michigan have the best opportunity to get to know these representatives of America's most primitive bird order. Loons are most likely detected on northern lakes at dusk or after dark by their yodel-like calls (which signal territorial ownership). This maniacal "laugh," coupled with the myth that the moon can cause lunacy, explains their name. These two-and-a-half to three foot long divers are often noticed when they are well out in a lake. They ride low in the water with their bill somewhat raised and, when in breeding plumage, they are unmistakable from their black and white checkered backs. An identification challenge arises following the breeding season, however, when they molt into a drab, brownish color. Though they scatter to deep lakes and reservoirs throughout the Midwest on their way to the Gulf Coast, they do not call and usually go unnoticed.

Common Loons eat live fish, which they detect by swimming about with their necks craned so that their eyes are beneath the surface. When a fish is located, they propel themselves rapidly downward by stroking their huge, webbed feet simultaneously. Their feet are located well back on the body to increase swimming skill. However, this adaptation causes them to be so awkward that they rarely venture onto land.

By the time of their return trip to the northland in March and April, Common Loons have taken on their summertime colors. However, males rarely call until back on their breeding territories in May, and so still tend to escape notice. Nesting ensues in June. Nests are masses of damp vegetation placed at the water's edge near deep drop offs. Most clutches contain only two eggs, which are bronze-olive and darkly speckled. Incubation is performed by both parents and requires 28 days. The downy young are able to swim soon after hatching but require parental feeding until a few weeks of age. Young ride on the backs of their swimming parents.

The Common Loon is the State Bird of Minnesota.

IDENTIFICATION TIPS

▶ great size and blue-gray color
   overall; adults have a white
   coloration around their heads;
   underparts are darker

▶ their call is a series of deep
   hoarse croaks

GREAT BLUE HERON

Ardea herodias

North America's largest herons stand three-feet tall and have wings spanning six feet. Their broad wings beat in a deep, slow cadence that attests to their size, while their legs trail out behind. Except when just landing and taking off, their heads are folded back on their necks in an S shape, a posture that distinguishes them from cranes. Great Blue Herons are sometimes erroneously called cranes; however, the only cranes in North America are much less common.

Great Blue Herons are usually encountered while they are standing statuesquely in the shallows of a stream or lake, waiting for a fish to swim within striking range. Quarry, which can also include frogs and even field mice, is taken with surprising swiftness. After being speared, fish are juggled around to be swallowed headfirst so that spines do not impede the process. Amazingly large fish can sometimes be seen moving down a heron's throat as the bird retches.

Having wintered at latitudes with open water, Great Blue Herons arrive back at their nesting colonies just after ice-breakup. After seeing them as solitary hunters, it is surprising to witness how social they become at nest sites. Their two- to three-foot-wide stick nests are closely spaced through the spreading crowns of a few huge trees. At each, a courting pair fans the filamentous plumes on their heads, necks, and backs. As nest refurbishing gets underway, each nesting pair croaks, squawks, and spars viciously with six-inch bills with their neighbors. Despite apparent havoc, the mutual protection offered by the colony lessens nest raiding by Blue Jays and American Crows.

Incubation of their three to six pale-blue eggs takes place in March, well before their riverbottom forest habitat has leafed out. The parents take turns sitting on the eggs during the month-long incubation period. Both parents feed the chicks partially-digested fish during April through June as the young birds grow in the nest. Frightened chicks sometimes regurgitate this gruel onto people who have the misfortune of wandering in beneath the colony.

Following nesting, Great Blue Herons scatter across the countryside to favorable fishing spots such as streams, marshes, farm ponds, and flooded ditches. They are sometimes joined at these areas by Great Egrets (*Ardea alba*), waders of similar size and shape whose feathers are pure white.

IDENTIFICATION TIPS

▶ soars in wide circles, with wings in a shallow V shape
▶ when overhead, the blackish wings are of two tones (the flight feathers are paler)
▶ while soaring, they will often rock and tilt unsteadily
▶ their naked heads are relatively small
▶ eagles have larger heads, shorter tails, and their wings lay flat when soaring

TURKEY VULTURE

Cathartes aura

Commonly called "buzzards," these impressive birds are usually seen wheeling lazily overhead. Where one is seen, there are normally others scattered through the sky, apparently relying on each other to find food. Their wings span six feet, as compared to a Red-tailed Hawk's four, and they are held in a distinctive shallow V shape. Turkey Vultures are further distinguished by their black plumage, except for their silvery underwing. Turkey Vultures fly so effortlessly that they are able to spend hours simply gliding aloft, especially during the warmest part of the day when updraft and thermals provide them the greatest lift. On the rare occasions that they do flap their wings, the beats are surprisingly deep and slow.

Although Turkey Vultures are usually high in the sky, they sometimes swoop low over the land while tilting rapidly from side to side to maintain stability. This enables them to use odor in addition to vision in locating carrion. Unlike most birds, vultures have an excellent sense of smell as evidenced by their large nostrils and the over-sized olfactory lobes of their brains. Hungry vultures are sometimes misled by the smell of mushrooms and stagnant water. Natural gas companies have used circling vultures to locate leaks in pipelines.

Today's landscape and the prevalence of road kills apparently favor Turkey Vultures, as they remain common. Their food habits provide a purifying service as they remove diseased carcasses from the landscape. They are adapted for this lifestyle by being immune to diseases such as Salmonellosis and Botulism. Their bare heads reduce contamination of decaying material. It is the bare head that resulted in their common name, as in this way they resemble Wild Turkeys.

Turkey Vultures are with us from March through September, often roosting together at night in large trees in sheltered valleys. Eggs are laid in March, typically in dark places such as shelter caves, hollow logs, stumps, and abandoned buildings. Incubation of their one to three white eggs requires about one month. Although adults are voiceless, nestlings are able to hiss. When frightened, they also vomit through their nostrils, a sight and smell no doubt discouraging to many would-be predators. At the age of two to three months, the adult-sized young reluctantly leave the nest.

IDENTIFICATION TIPS
- ▶ white phase: solid white with black wing tips; often rust-stained on head; bill and feet pink
- ▶ blue phase: bluish body with a white head; wings paler
- ▶ blue phase is abundant in the eastern Great Plains, but uncommon east of the Mississippi River

SNOW GOOSE

Chen caerulescens

ne of the most memorable wildlife wonders in the Midwest is the migration of Snow Geese. Usually the first evidence that there are geese overhead are numerous faint cries, like the distant barking of dogs. Looking up, white speckles may be seen, wending in vees and lines high against the azure sky. During prime migration periods, several flocks containing hundreds each may pass over in a single day. Always a harbinger of the changing seasons, fall flights are typically on bright, late fall days when there is a bite to the wind. In spring, migration can precede the disappearance of snow and ice, and seems so urgent that the geese sometimes continue flying and honking through the night.

These are medium-sized geese, about 30 inches in length, including their long necks. They weigh five to six pounds. Typical Snow Geese are white with black wingtips. Mixed with most flocks, especially through the mid-continent, are a few individuals with blue-gray bodies and white heads and necks. "Blue geese" were formerly thought to be a separate species, but recognized in 1983 to be simply a color-phase of Snow Geese. "Snows" and "blues" were perhaps separated by the last glaciation and may have been on their way to becoming independent species. During their first year of life, those of the "snow geese" color-phase are dusty white, while "blue geese" are entirely gray-brown.

If near the open fields and wetlands where they land to rest and feed, these exciting waterfowl can be even more impressive. Especially on national wildlife refuge wetlands, they can become so amassed as to exceed 50,000 individuals per acre, and some areas have held over a half-million birds at one time. These staging areas offer aquatic foods plus the security provided by reeds and surrounding water. The geese disperse from the areas daily to graze on green shoots in surrounding pastures and wheatfields, and eat the leftovers in the stubble of harvested corn, soybeans, rice, or sorghum. Each night they return to the safety of wetlands until freeze-up forces them farther south. They winter in favorable spots from southern Iowa to the Gulf Coast.

Snow Geese nest colonially on the tundra of the high Arctic from the shores of Hudson Bay northward through the Baffin Islands. The clutch of two to six white eggs requires 24 days of incubation. The precocial young grow rapidly and are flying when barely beyond a month of age. High reproductive rates and excellent survival through the year have enabled Snow Geese populations to thrive.

IDENTIFICATION TIPS
▶ black head and neck contrast with pale breast and the broad white chinstrap that runs onto the side of the head
▶ sexes look alike
▶ migrate by day and night
▶ there are 6 recognized subspecies, which differ greatly in size but only slightly in color

Canada Goose
Branta canadensis

These legendary "wild geese" have lost much of their allure in recent decades because of their increasing tendency to live in proximity to people. At one time, they were the mysterious "honkers" seen overhead en route to some far off land. Now, throughout much of the country, they flock like noisy poultry along lakes in parks and on golf courses. It is the combination of water and mown lawns that attracts Canada Geese, as they are among the few birds able to digest cellulose-rich material such as grass. Like their mammalian counterparts, cattle, they must graze almost constantly to derive their needed nutrition.

Though increasingly familiar, Canada Geese remain impressive. Those individuals that remain year-round to nest in the Midwest are "Giant" Canada Geese, a race in which the males, or ganders, can weigh nearly 20 pounds and have a wingspan of six feet. Females are slightly smaller. Historically, cliff nesters in Missouri and elsewhere in the Midwest, "Giants" were brought from the brink of extinction with the placement of nesting tubs in ponds, and by releases throughout the country. "Interior" Canada Geese, another race of the species, are one-third smaller than "Giants" and remain the "wild goose" of lore, flying over us to nest in extreme northern Canada.

Flocks typically fly in V-formations while emitting deep two-syllabled *hu-onks*. Male-female bonds are permanent, and the pair often travels with young from the previous year until ready to nest the following spring. The female constructs a nest lined with down from her own breast and commonly lays five to six cream-colored eggs. Resident "Giant" Canada Geese lay eggs as early as March. Once incubation begins, the goose rarely leaves her nest for the 25 to 28 days required for the young to hatch. The gander stands guard and courageously attacks any creature he perceives as a threat. Newly-hatched young are precocial, which means that they are covered with down and able to follow their parents and feed soon after hatching. They grow quickly, and are able to fly by mid-summer.

IDENTIFICATION TIPS

▶ in flight, the white belly contrasts with the dark breast and wings

▶ long square tail, short neck, large head

▶ females are dull-colored but have distinctive white eye patch

▶ no other duck has the long, slicked-back crest

▶ rapid flight; they dodge easily between trees

WOOD DUCK

Aix sponsa

rake Wood Ducks are considered by many to be the most beautiful of America's waterfowl. Hens, though less spectacular, are readily identified by white patches around the eye, and spotted breasts. Both sexes have tufts down the back of their necks and unusually long, square tails, that are especially obvious in flight. It is perhaps this feature that helps them to maneuver through trees and brake with surprising abruptness when landing on a branch. When flushed, they take off with whistling wings and a squealing, rising *oo-eek, oo-eek*. This apparently helps them to maintain contact with each other when flying through woods.

True to their name, these common ducks live along wooded shores and in forested bottomlands throughout their range. Though spotted occasionally in the far west and northern Rockies, their primary range extends from the Atlantic and Gulf coasts west to Oklahoma, Kansas, and the Dakotas, and north into portions of Canada. In winter, they retreat to the southern states where waterways remain open. Unlike most flocking ducks, Wood Ducks only occasionally group up, usually in shallowly-flooded timber where there is a banquet of aquatic invertebrates, succulent greenery, roots, seeds, and acorns.

Courting drakes swim near potential mates while tilting and turning about. This begins as early as late summer, and upon arriving on nesting grounds the following spring, most will have been paired off for months. Wood Ducks are one of a few waterfowl to nest in tree cavities, typically in holes left by broken branches or in large excavations created by woodpeckers. Laying commences in April or May and one white egg is laid each day. When the clutch of up to 15 eggs is complete, the hen initiates incubation so they hatch fairly synchronously about a month later.

Usually the morning after hatching, the hen begins clucking on the ground beneath the tree to entice her ducklings to jump from the nesting cavity. They may fall as far as 60 feet onto the hard ground without injury. When they are assembled, their mother sets off with them scrambling after her to find the nearest water. This journey, which may be as far as several hundred yards, is the most hazardous phase of their lives. Once in water, the tiny ducklings may still fall prey to bullfrogs, snapping turtles, and herons. Their mother may attempt to lure predators away from them with a broken wing act. Wood Ducks nest only once a year, and will use nest boxes.

IDENTIFICATION TIPS

▶ male is easily recognized by the glossy green head and white neck ring; body is grayish with a rusty chest

▶ female is mottled brown with a whitish tail

▶ both sexes have a violet-blue speculum that is bordered on both sides with white; in flight, these white bars and the blue speculum are visible

♂

♀

MALLARD
Anas platyrhynchos

allards are the best-known and possibly the most abundant ducks in the world. Mallards from Europe are the ancestors of almost all domestic ducks. Domestic Mallards sometimes revert to the wild and even cross with wild Mallards. Wild Mallards, however, can usually be recognized by their skittish behavior and tendency to form large flocks in fall and winter. They range nearly throughout North America. Drakes are sometimes called "green heads," especially by hunters. Hens are plain brown. Both sexes have a patch of blue-green secondary wing feathers, called a speculum, that shows in flight. Adults are about two feet in length when the neck is out-stretched, and they weigh two-and-a-half pounds. The Mallard's voice is the familiar, nasal quack.

Mallards are members of a group called dabbling ducks (also known as marsh or puddle ducks) — ducks that feed in shallow water by tipping in to take plants, seeds, and invertebrates from the bottom. Dabbling ducks are able to take off vertically, while other ducks must run across the water before becoming airborne. Mallards tend to winter in large flocks in sheltered coves of lakes and other wetlands throughout much of the central United States. Wintering birds range as far north as South Dakota and Iowa depending on the availability of open water.

Northward migration commences as early as February. Springtime observers of the ducks that visit nearby ponds are entertained by courtship chases and displays. The greatest extent of the breeding range lies in the prairie provinces of Canada. Once mating occurs, females are left to the incubation and rearing chores while both sexes go through a mid- to late-summer molt that renders them flightless for a few weeks. A hen may lay as many as a dozen eggs in a down-lined nest. Those nests in the northern prairie region may be surprisingly distant from water. In less remote regions, hens often select unnatural nest sites such as planters, stone walls, and window wells. Eggs are buff-colored and require about 28 days of incubation. The young are precocial.

Mallards from the north are rather late fall migrants in the Midwest, and are our most popular of game waterfowl. Waterfowl observers in the more eastern parts of the Midwest are likely to see the American Black Duck (*Anas rubripes*), which often flocks with mallards, and in which both sexes resemble a dark female Mallard.

IDENTIFICATION TIPS

▶ both sexes have a pale blue area on the front edge of the wings

▶ male has a distinctive white facial crescent

▶ female is brown, mottled; late in the year, males may resemble females

▶ in flight, teal are recognized by their small size and tight flocks

▶ in flight, male Blue-wings show dark bellies, while Green-winged Teal show white bellies

▶ female Blue-wings are larger and longer billed than female Green-wings

♂

♀

BLUE-WINGED TEAL

Anas discors

These small ducks are more likely seen than others because their migration through the Midwest takes place during the warmer parts of the spring and fall when people are more often enjoying the outdoors. Their name derives from the powder-blue patch on their wings, which is seen best in flight. Drakes have a diagnostic "half moon" on the face. Hens, because they alone provide parental care, are true to the duck pattern of being cryptically-colored so that they are less detectable when on the nest. Blue-wings are 15 inches long with neck outstretched and weigh about a pound. They are swift fliers, often forming compact flocks that course back and forth over a marsh before finally determining that they are clear for a landing. As dabbling ducks, they favor shallow marshes where they swim about and tip in to reach seeds, tender shoots, aquatic insects, and tiny crustaceans. When disturbed, they spring directly into flight with a flutter while emitting peeping sounds.

Though most known as spring and fall migrants, Blue-wings breed in association with wetlands throughout the majority of the Midwest. Their breeding range extends northward through the prairie provinces of Canada, a region that supplies the majority of the fall migrants. Compared to other ducks, Blue-wings are unusually early fall migrants, most moving through during September. This early migration occurs because, unlike most ducks, many Blue-wings travel all the way to Peru, Brazil, and Argentina to winter. Upon their return in March and April, most Blue-wings have paired off. Nests are constructed on dry ground near water and concealed from above by arching vegetation. Ten to 13 cream-colored eggs constitute a clutch. The hen incubates them until they hatch in 23 to 24 days and then leads her precocial ducklings to water.

Blue-winged Teal are slightly larger than their cousins, Green-winged Teal (*Anas crecca*), which lack the blue shoulder and are much later migrants in Fall.

IDENTIFICATION TIPS

▶ their long wings are held in an arched position; the crook is marked with black which confirms identification

▶ the head is mainly white, suggesting a Bald Eagle, but it has a broad black cheek patch

▶ in flight, they flap more than they sail; wingbeats are slow and deep

▶ call is a series of loud, clear whistles

▶ North America's only raptor that plunges into the water to catch fish

OSPREY

Pandion haliaetus

lthough less common than many of the birds in this book, Ospreys are conspicuous both physically and behaviorally. When in the air, they are usually noticed because of their long wings, which span five feet and arch like a gull's with a dark patch at the bend. The body of the bird is about 2 feet long. Though primarily white below, their wings and tail are barred with brown. Ospreys are dark brown above. They have dark masks across their yellow eyes.

Also called "fish hawks," Ospreys fly over ponds, lakes, and streams by alternately gliding and flapping. Upon sighting a fish near the surface, they may hover briefly before diving from as high as 100 feet to plunge into the water feet first. Once a fish is securely grasped by the feet, they carry it from the water, repositioning it so that the head is forward and thus more aerodynamic. Ospreys will typically wiggle in flight to shake water from their feathers.

Ospreys are one of few species to range around the world. Although they can be found in any state during their spring and fall migration, their breeding range extends across the northern states and southern Canada, and along both coasts. The majority winter in South America. One satellite-tracked individual that left St. Paul, Minnesota, in September was found at weekly intervals in Missouri, Texas, Mexico, Costa Rica, Venezuela, Peru and, finally, Bolivia, where it made its winter home.

Like other members of the raptor family, Ospreys build large, stick nests. They lay two to four heavily splotched white eggs which are incubated for 30 to 35 days entirely by the female. Her mate delivers food while she is on the nest and helps her to feed the rapidly growing eyasses (raptor nestlings). A brood of three requires six pounds of fish daily. Young Ospreys fly from the nest when two to three months of age.

IDENTIFICATION TIPS

▶ adults can't be missed with their white heads, white tails, and huge size

▶ bill is yellow and massive

▶ dark immatures have dusky heads and tails, with a darker bill; they usually have a fair amount of white in the wing linings and on the breast

▶ soars on flattened wings

BALD EAGLE
Haliaeetus leucocephalus

Our National Bird is known to all despite being only occasionally sighted in the wild. They are a migratory species that nests in association with lakes and streams during the summer months in the northern Midwest. During the coldest part of the winter they migrate to the southern Midwest where they are most likely seen along major rivers and the unfrozen parts of lakes.

Typically, Bald Eagles perch high in shoreline trees to keep a lookout for prey and to avoid disturbance. In this prominent location, their diagnostic white head and tail are eye-catching, contrasting vividly with their dark brown body. At nearly three feet in length and weighing up to 15 pounds, their size is difficult to judge until they are in the air. It is then that their deep, plodding wing-beats attest to their size. When they set their wings to soar, they exhibit an airplane-like profile that spans seven feet.

As white-headed adults, Bald Eagles are one of the easiest birds to identify. Individuals younger than five years, however, lack the white head and tail and vary from being solid dark brown to being blotched throughout with white. These juveniles, which are otherwise similar to adults in size, habitat, and behavior, compose about one-third of the eagle population. Wintering flocks typically contain both age groups.

Fish compose most of the Bald Eagle's diet. When a fish is sighted, the predator will swoop low over the water to dip its powerful, sharp-taloned feet beneath the surface to snag prey. Opportunists, they also scavenge for dead fish on shores and the dead and dying ducks and geese that result from large concentrations of migrating waterfowl. Bald Eagles will also scavenge road-side kills.

Bald Eagles build the largest nest of any bird. Composed of sticks, nests typically exceed three feet across and two feet in depth. Nests are situated on strong branches near the tops of huge trees, and are perennial, meaning that the eagles will return to the same nest each year and continue to build and reconstruct it. Some eagles have been known to use the same nest for over 35 years. Two to three white eggs are laid in March, hatch in April, and the young fledge in June. Since the banning of DDT in 1972, Bald Eagles are nesting more commonly in the Midwest.

SHARP-SHINNED HAWK
- ▶ small, slim hawk with short, rounded wings and long tail
- ▶ flies with several quick beats and a glide
- ▶ Cooper's Hawk is obviously larger with a rounded tail; Sharp-shin tail is narrower and more square-cut
- ▶ male Cooper's and female Sharp-shin resemble each other closely making identification difficult

AMERICAN TREE SPARROW
- ▶ the large central breast spot and a solid red-brown cap distinguish these sparrows from others
- ▶ bill is dark above, yellow below
- ▶ two white wingbars
- ▶ seen in large flocks in winter

Sharp-shinned Hawk
Accipiter striatus

American Tree Sparrow
Spizella arborea

Sharp-shinned Hawks are small, slim woodland hawks that are adapted to prey on other birds. They have fairly short, rounded wings, and long tails. These features enable bursts of speed and maneuverability when pursuing small birds among branches. When perched, the tail extends several inches beyond the tip of the folded wings. Sharp-shinned Hawks average 11 inches in length with females being about one-third larger than males. As adults, their upper parts are blue-gray and their breasts, bellies, and shanks are barred with flecks of orangish-brown. Their tails are boldly barred and their eyes are orange. Juveniles, which seem nearly as common as adults, have brown backs flecked with white, and streaks of brown on their otherwise light breasts. Juveniles have finely barred tails and yellow eyes. Both age groups have bright yellow legs.

These reclusive hawks are perhaps best known because of their habit of frequenting neighborhoods where bird feeders concentrate small birds, thus making predation easy. They are difficult to pick out among the branches until the moment of the ambush. Captured prey is taken to a favorite perch, called a "butcher block," where the predator, while furtively glancing about for thieves, quickly de-feathers and consumes it.

Sharp-shinned Hawks and their look-alike larger relative, the Cooper's Hawk (*Accipiter cooperii*), are migratory but reside in the southern Midwest year-round. Sharp-shinned Hawks build stick nests, usually well-concealed in evergreens. The males do nearly all of the hunting during incubation and into the nestling stage. Four to five white eggs (often marked with brown) typically hatch in June, and the young depart the nest a month later.

American Tree Sparrows are winter visitors from the far north. They are five-and-a-half inches in length and identified by their rusty cap, wingbars, and the dark central spot on their plain gray breast. Flocks of them inhabit weedy fields and brushy wastelands during their winter stay.

American Tree Sparrow   Sharp-shinned Hawk

IDENTIFICATION TIPS

▶ large; broad-winged; round-tailed

▶ whitish breast, broad band of streaks across belly

▶ call is a high scream, often imitated by jays

RED-TAILED HAWK

Buteo jamaicensis

 ed-tailed Hawks are by far the most commonly seen bird of prey in North America. These are large, open-country hawks. No matter the season, it is possible to hear their thin, raspy screams and see one or two circling overhead with broad wings set and tail fanned. From below, the tail appears solidly tan unless the sun shines through it or the bird tips, revealing its reddish upper side. With wings spanning four feet and a length approaching two feet, Red-tailed Hawks are impressive whether soaring or perched.

When these familiar birds of prey are on poles along highways, it is usually their gleaming white breasts that catch the eye first. Most have a band of dark flecks across the belly. There is great color variation among individuals however. Some are nearly solid brown, except for the tail, and some are nearly white. Even tail color is not a conclusive identifier because those younger than two years of age have finely barred tails on a brown or rusty background.

Red-tailed Hawks prey primarily on mice, rabbits, ground squirrels, and snakes, animals often found in grasslands. They are most conspicuous in winter because they gravitate to grassy roadsides where people are most likely to see them. Additionally, individuals from the northern breeding range have migrated south and add to the more southern, year-round population. They pair up in late winter and by late February or March, each pair begins construction of a nest, typically in the high crotch of a large tree along a woodland edge. Their stick nests, two to three feet across and up to two feet deep, are easy to see before leaf-out. Fittingly, those nests in the cornbelt states are often lined with corn husks.

Eggs are laid in early March. The usual clutch contains two to three eggs. They are chicken-egg-sized, dirty-white and speckled with brown. The month-long incubation is done entirely by the female, usually during March. Her mate feeds her on the nest. The heads of the downy young may be first seen above the nest rim in April, and they fledge during late May and June.

AMERICAN KESTREL

Falco sparverius

Our smallest falcons are easily seen because they tend to perch on power lines along roadways. They are recognized by their blunt-headed, neckless profile and rather long tails. In flight, they exhibit the relatively long, pointed wings characteristic of falcons. Males, which among falcons are the smallest of the two sexes, are nine inches in length and gaudily-colored with blue wings and orangish backs and tails. Females are nearly a foot in length and lack the blue on the wings and the brilliant russet coloration. Both sexes have a vertical black bar on the side of the head and a black "whisker" extending down from the bill. Like other raptors, they have sharp talons for holding the prey and a hooked bill for tearing it apart.

American Kestrels reside in grasslands where the vegetation is tall enough to accommodate mice and voles, their most common prey, but short enough to see them moving about. They drop swiftly onto prey from a perch or from a hovering point in the sky. They also eat large insects, snakes, lizards, and frogs. They rarely employ their falcon speed to take small birds. Their alternate name, "Sparrowhawk," is more fitting for the Sharp-shinned Hawk.

American Kestrels nest northward to the tree line in Canada and spend the winter throughout all but the northern parts of the Midwest. It is during the winter that they are most conspicuous. This is partly because they gravitate to the habitat provided by roadside rights-of-way when not nesting. Also, migrants from the north join those that reside at the lower latitudes year round, resulting in a larger population in the Midwest.

Beginning in April, flying pairs emit *killy killy killy* cries as they pair off for the upcoming nesting season. While migrants depart for the north, residents move to areas in the vicinity where there are cavities for nesting. In addition to holes in trees, they select niches in walls and specially-designed kestrel boxes. They use little to no nesting material. The female lays four to five brown, speckled eggs. They hatch in a month and the young fledge a month later. Pairs will sometimes raise a second brood later in the summer.

IDENTIFICATION TIPS

▶ long, sweeping, pointed tail and short rounded wings (both sexes)

▶ runs swiftly; flight strong with a noisy takeoff

▶ male has a white neck-ring (although it is not always visible)

RING-NECKED PHEASANT
Phasianus colchicus

Rooster Ring-necked Pheasants are gloriously colored and, although chicken-sized, exceed 30 inches in length because of their long tail. Hens are roughly two-thirds their size and amazingly plain in comparison. Pheasants seem especially fitting for the fall of the year because their golds and bronzes blend with the russets of crispy leaves, and their nervous alertness seems suited for the brisk weather. Also, fall is the season when hunters renew their acquaintance with this wily bird. Masters at hiding, pheasants can explode into flight at the last possible moment with a commotion of fluttering wings and croaks that startle even the most prepared hunters. They accelerate rapidly and when safely out of range, intermittently glide and beat their wings for as far as a mile.

It is appropriate that Ring-necks are best known as game birds because that is the primary reason for them being in North America. Believed to be native to the Orient, Ring-necked Pheasants spread across Europe during the Roman Era. Early attempts to establish them in North America, including George Washington's releases at Mount Vernon in the 1770s, were met with failure. They first took hold in Oregon in the 1880s and in the Midwest a few years later. By 1930, they had come to occupy most of their current Midwestern range, which extends through the Cornbelt from Ohio to Nebraska and the Dakotas and the prairie provinces of Canada. They are absent from northern coniferous and eastern deciduous forests and, seemingly deterred by heat and humidity, fade out to the south of Iowa and mid-Ohio.

These familiar farmland bids are especially plentiful where there is a mixture of row-crops in which to find grain, and grasslands in which to nest. From May through June, roosters select open spots from which to court hens with loud, two-syllabled, croaking calls followed by a rapid clapping of wings. They extend wings to show off their splendid feathers and even fight each other for mates using the spurs on the backs of their legs. Hens lay 12 to 16 olive-cream eggs in nests of grass and leaves. Nests are placed in hayfields, idle acres, road ditches, and the odd weedy corners of crop fields. Chicks hatch in 24 days and soon set about to find food with their mothers. The early emergence of wing feathers enables them to fly when still very small, at only two weeks of age.

Ring-necked Pheasants are the State Bird of South Dakota.

IDENTIFICATION TIPS

▶ females are smaller than males, with a smaller
head; they are less iridescent and less likely to
have a beard

WILD TURKEY
Meleagris gallopavo

By weight, these are the largest birds native to North America. Adult males, or gobblers, often exceed 20 pounds. Though they spend much of their time on the ground, turkeys can fly—and seeing such a large object in the air is impressive. Their flight is of short duration and lumbering. They roost in trees at night, often as a group.

In addition to their large size, Wild Turkeys are unique in many ways. Their heads are essentially bare and the flesh varies from gray to blue to red. Turkeys possess a larger number of tail feathers than most birds, and their body feathers reflect metallic gold. Most males and some females have "beards," a cord of fibers extending from the center of the breast that may be a foot in length. Males have spurs on their legs that are longest on older birds.

Because of their size, delicious meat, and elusive behavior, Wild Turkeys are prized game birds. Not only were they favored as game by native Americans, but they were one of few North American birds to be domesticated. The Anasazi of the American Southwest kept them hundreds of years ago as a source of feathers for clothing. Turkeys were introduced to western Europe around the year 1530, at a time when similar exotic items were being brought from Asia Minor. Thus, there may be a connection between the bird and the country of the same name.

Wild Turkeys are non-migratory. As the result of introductions and management, their range has expanded northward in recent years, and they now occupy woodland borders throughout much of the Midwest.

Courtship strutting by males, during which they *gobble* and fan their tails, commences in February and continues through May. Strutting is most intense at daybreak. Display areas are usually in open fields. Sometimes several females and strutting males are seen together. Males are polygamous. As hens become receptive, they breed, then travel some distance to lay eggs in shallow nests on the ground, usually at the edge of a field or in a clearing in the woods. Incubation of the 8 to 15 buff-colored, lightly-speckled eggs requires 28 days. Broods of young follow their mothers as they grow during the summer. Often two or three broods group together forming flocks of up to two dozen that persist through the winter.

The Wild Turkey almost became the National Bird of the United States, losing by one vote in a congressional ballot.

IDENTIFICATION TIPS

▶ small, rotund

▶ reddish-brown with a short, gray tail; about the size of a Meadowlark

▶ male is identified by the white throat and eye line; these areas are buff-colored in females

▶ ruffed grouse is larger with a fan-like tail

▶ avoids deep forests

NORTHERN BOBWHITE

Colinus virginianus

These exciting game birds measure about eight inches in length and have short, rapidly-beating wings to carry their one-third pound weight. Females are distinguished from males by having tan in place of white on the eye-line and throat. Quail, as they are usually called, are most often detected by sound during their spring and summer nesting season. Their two-parted whistle was for some reason said to match the words "bob white," and the name stuck. Occasionally these whistlers, which tend to be unmated males, are seen on fenceposts or other prominent locations. Or a pair might be seen together, running ahead of a car along country lanes, darting into and out of bordering vegetation.

Bobwhites are most thrilling during the fall and winter when a person happens to bust a covey and suddenly finds a dozen or more of them springing into flight and coursing away in all directions, wings whirring. This experience is a large part of the allure and challenge of quail hunting. Later, soft calls may be heard from the brush as the covey members attempt to reunite. Covey formation is important because as a group, they are better able to find food and avoid predators. On sub-freezing nights, a covey of perhaps a dozen birds will huddle in a circle with heads outward.

Bobwhites are nonmigratory and essentially absent from the most northern states because of poor survival during especially frigid winters. Pairing occurs in March but nesting does not get underway until May. Nests are built directly on the ground and typically well-hidden among arching grasses. Unlike most chicken-like birds, both sexes build the nest and exchange incubation duties. Nests may contain 12 to 15 cream-colored eggs. They hatch in 23 to 24 days. The chicks are fuzzy, yellowish, and so tiny as to resemble bumble bees. Bobwhites may nest twice or, rarely, three times a season.

Bobwhites consume insects when growing and seeds and green shoots as adults. They associate with areas where agricultural grain fields, grasslands, and woody cover are in close proximity. Landscape changes, including larger fields and few brushy fence-lines, have caused populations to decline. Although vulnerable to severe winter and spring conditions, their high reproductive potential enables them to rebound where habitat is favorable.

IDENTIFICATION TIPS

▶ rather noisy, repetitive call

▶ 2 black upper breast bands; chick has 1 band

▶ in flight, displays orange on the upper tail and lower back, longish tail, white wing stripe

▶ tail is longer than other plovers

KILLDEER

Charadrius vociferus

he *kill-dee-kill-dee-kill-dee* cries of these common plovers can be heard between their arrival in March until their departure in October. Essentially white below and brown above, they are distinguished by two black bands across the upper chest. They run about rapidly on spindly legs, often stopping abruptly with a slight bow. Or they skip into flight and course low over the ground for a short distance before landing with a run. Their rusty rump can be seen when they are in low level flight. When overhead, the Killdeer's white undersides and long, pointed wings are reminiscent of a gull's.

These conspicuous birds frequent short-grass, gravelly, or barren areas such as closely-cropped pastures, driveways, and open construction sites. Though members of the shorebird family, they do not require a shoreline, although sometimes they are sighted on beaches and river gravel bars. Their primary foods, insects and worms, are more available where the earth is moist.

Killdeers build no nest but simply create a shallow depression for their eggs in a pebble substrate. Like many ground-nesting birds, Killdeers feign injury to lure predators from their nests and young. It is not unusual to hear their plaintive trill and see them floundering about on the ground when they believe their nest is threatened. This strategy is successful because the splotchy brown pattern of the eggs matches the gray, tan, or brown gravel on which they are laid. There are usually four eggs with pointy ends projecting inward to fit neatly together in a clutch. They hatch in 24 to 26 days.

The young are precocial and follow their parents soon after hatching, seeming little more than puff-balls on toothpicks. They freeze instinctively when danger arises. In a few weeks, they are on their own and the parent birds can nest a second time. Killdeers breed throughout most of North America and winter in the southern states and Mexico.

IDENTIFICATION TIPS

▶ complete black ring encircles yellow bill of adults

▶ similar to Herring Gull but smaller

▶ other larger eastern gulls have flesh-colored or black legs

RING-BILLED GULL

Larus delawarensis

These medium-sized gulls are perhaps the most frequently encountered inland gulls in the Midwest. They nest across the northern states and winter in association with rivers and reservoirs in the south. In between, they can be seen along almost any stream or lake. They are 16 inches long and have a wingspan of four feet. The name stems from the black ring around the tip of the adults' bills. Mature Ring-billed Gulls have white bodies, gray upper-parts, black wingtips, and yellow feet. Those younger than two years are mottled brown, have a black tip on a pinkish bill, and pink legs.

Ring-billed Gulls breed in colonies near water in areas with sparse vegetation. Each pair raises an average of two young each year. Ring-bills move south in late fall as waterways freeze over. Some remain in the north where spillways, power plants, and rapids keep water open. They eat small fish that come near the surface, and hundreds of individuals might be seen flying about or resting on the ice or water at especially favorable feeding areas. Opportunistic feeders, they also eat insects, earthworms, and human handouts. They often visit garbage dumps.

Many people think of gulls as "seagulls," and are surprised to learn of those associated with fresh water, such as Ring-billed Gulls. In reality, there are several kinds of gulls that visit the Midwest, mostly during spring, fall, and winter, including some more at home on the ocean. In fact, 19 of the world's 45 gull species have been sighted on the Mississippi River near St. Louis. Among those gulls occasionally seen by Midwesterners, Herring Gulls (*Larus argentatus*) are most noticeable because of their large size. They are especially plentiful around the Great Lakes and on large rivers. As adults, they have the same gray back, white body, black wingtip coloration as Ring-bills, but are nearly two feet in length and have a wingspan of four-and-a-half feet. Rather than a ring, they have a red dot on the bottom tip of the bill.

Small, black-headed gulls, Bonaparte's Gulls (*Larus philadelphia*) and Franklin's Gulls (*Larus pipixcan*) might be seen in the northern Midwest in summer and nearly everywhere in the Midwest during migration. The latter species commonly feeds in flocks behind plows.

IDENTIFICATION TIPS
▶ typical birds are gray with a whitish rump, two
  black wing bars, and a broad dark tail band;
  many color variations though

ROCK DOVE

Columba livia

igeons, as they are usually called, are familiar to all. Perhaps because they eat agricultural grains, they have lived in association with humans since the early days of civilization. Native to the Old World, some individuals first became domesticated over 3,000 years ago. Through selective breeding, they were developed into breeds specialized for food, visual appeal, and message delivery, such as homing pigeons. As the world has been explored and settled, pigeons have been transported about and have become feral nearly everywhere.

Caged pigeons were listed among the supplies brought to the Jamestown Colony in 1610, so they were introduced to the New World very early. They now range across North America with the exception of the far north. The various colors in current wild populations attest to their human-modified ancestry. The original wild-type — birds with charcoal bodies, light-gray wings, and two black wing bars — still predominates in the population.

Maintaining their close association with people, pigeon flocks are prevalent in cities, towns, and on farms. Superb fliers, they course through the sky at over 60 miles per hour. Common flight displays include clapping the wing-tips over the back and gliding with wings held in a V. To impress females, males strut about, puff their crops, fan their tails, stretch, bow and rotate in place, while emitting a rolling *coo*.

Courtship and nesting can occur during all but the coldest weeks of the year. Nesting colonies are usually in man-made structures including niches on buildings, under bridges, and in barns. Their two white eggs require 20 days of incubation. Squabs are fed a regurgitated "pigeon milk" by both parents during the month that they are growing in the nest. Soon after fledging their young, or sometimes before, the pair begins nesting again.

IDENTIFICATION TIPS
▶ smaller and slimmer than Rock Doves
▶ pointed tail with large white spots

MOURNING DOVE

Zenaida macroura

he Midwest's native dove lives in a broad array of habitats from suburban yards to rural fields. They measure 10 to 12 inches in length, have a buff-gray plumage, a relatively small head, and pointed tail. Comparatively numerous, they are readily seen along roadways as they perch on power lines or pick up bits of sand to aid digestion of grains and seeds. Startled birds burst into flight, flaring the white outer feathers of their tails as their wings whistle. The whistling is also heard as they brake for a landing. Their soft, four- to five-parted *coo*, given from a perch, seems distant and melancholy, giving this dove its name.

After returning from the southern states in February and March, Mourning Doves prepare for mating by cooing, mutual preening, and billing — a behavior involving the interlocking of bills. Males embark on courtship flights in which they clap their wingtips together during exaggerated flaps as they gain altitude. Then they set their wings and glide downward through a long course that takes them back to the female and their chosen nest site.

Nests are typically built in the forks of horizontal branches. Pines seem preferred. The female constructs the nest by fitting sticks around herself that the male delivers by landing directly on her back. Two eggs are standard. They are white and sometimes visible from beneath through thin nests. Parents take turns sitting on the eggs. It takes two weeks for the eggs to hatch and another two weeks for the young to fly. As with Rock Doves, Mourning Dove nestlings are fed "pigeon milk." Pairs will nest two to four times during a season.

Pairs may be seen flying together well beyond the nesting season due to their strong, enduring bonds. Doves form flocks in fall and migration commences in the northern states in September. Some doves linger in the southern Midwest even into winter. Wintering doves sometimes visit bird feeding stations, favoring cracked corn that is scattered on the ground.

- ▶ slender, brown back, plain white breast
- ▶ rust color in the wings
- ▶ large white spots at tips of black tail feathers (most noticeable below)
- ▶ slightly curved bill, yellow lower beak

YELLOW-BILLED CUCKOO

Coccyzus americanus

Although many people know the "rain crow" by call, few know it by sight or by its official name, Yellow-billed Cuckoo. Cuckoos are vocal on even the warmest and most humid days, perhaps giving rise to the belief that they forecast rain. Their lazy, eight to ten note call begins with a *ka-ka-ka* and ends in a hollow-sounding *kowlp-kowlp-kowlp*. Or, it gives soft, evenly spaced *coos* in a series of five to ten. Though the sound seems distant, a person that takes the time to look might be surprised to find the slender, long-tailed, 11-inch bird nearby. Careful observation will discern the contrasting black and white bars on the under-tail, rust on the outer wing feathers, and the yellow lower bill. The latter feature distinguishes it from the Black-billed Cuckoo (*Coccyzus erythropthalmus*), also present in the Midwest. Additionally, the Black-billed Cuckoo's call is different, being a rapid series of three to four *coos*.

Yellow-billed Cuckoos are most common in the southern reaches of the Midwest. They arrive on breeding grounds in May, favoring thickets and forest edges, especially along streams. Their flight is slow, low and direct, frequently resulting in collisions with cars and house windows. Yellow-billed Cuckoos are one of few birds that eat hairy and spiny caterpillars. In fact, they eat them so regularly that the inner surfaces of their stomachs are furry as a result of the many spines that have pierced the lining. Cuckoos build flimsy, stick nests, usually in trees. They typically raise one to two broods each summer, laying three to four blue-green eggs per clutch. When food is most abundant, such as during webworm outbreaks, they may lay three clutches per season containing up to five eggs each. Because of the rapid development of their young — only 11 days of incubation and an additional nine days to fledging — cuckoos seem adapted to be brood parasites as are Brown-headed Cowbirds and the Old World cuckoos. American cuckoos, however, rarely lay their eggs in the nests of other birds.

IDENTIFICATION TIPS

▶ no other eared owl is bright red-brown

▶ young birds may lack conspicuous ears

▶ all other eastern "eared" owls are obviously larger

EASTERN SCREECH-OWL

Otus asio

astern Screech-Owls are the smallest of our common North American owls. They range from seven to nine inches in length and, because of the "ear" tufts, resemble miniature Great Horned Owls. As with most nocturnal creatures, it is their sound that reveals their presence. Their most common vocalization is a long, descending *whinny*. They also deliver an even-toned trill and, when agitated, the piercing scream that has given them their name.

Eastern Screech-Owls come in two color phases, rusty and gray. Rusty individuals predominate across the mid-latitudes of their range from Missouri and Arkansas eastward. Gray forms are more common elsewhere. When rusty and gray owls mate, their individual offspring are either one phase or the other, not a blend of the two. Eastern Screech-Owls range from the East Coast to the Rocky Mountains, where the look-alike Western Screech-Owl (*Otus kennicottii*) takes over.

These small owls live in tree-dominated landscapes, whether forests, wood lots, or city yards. Extremely nocturnal, they catch mice that become active after dark and take small birds from night roosts. Insects, crayfish, and earthworms constitute much of their diet during the warmer months of the year. They are nonmigratory.

Eastern Screech-Owls nest in tree hollows and in lofts and niches of farm buildings, a behavior that regularly puts them in competition with squirrels and European Starlings. Egg-laying occurs from March to June, with a clutch containing as many as six white eggs. The male feeds the incubating female during the latter days of the month-long incubation period. Because incubation begins with the first egg laid, the eggs hatch over sequential days and the young are noticeably different in size. They typically depart the nesting cavity in the order that they were hatched at about one month of age.

AMERICAN CROW
- ▶ large, chunky, completely black bird, glossed with purplish cast in strong sunlight
- ▶ Common Raven is larger; has a wedge-shaped tail

GREAT HORNED OWL
- ▶ large, with ear tufts or "horns"
- ▶ heavily barred beneath
- ▶ has a conspicuous white throat bib
- ▶ twice the size of the crows that often harass it

GREAT HORNED OWL
Bubo virginianus

AMERICAN CROW
Corvus brachyrhynchos

arge, powerful predators of the night, Great Horned Owls are the Midwest's largest, common owls. They are one-and-a-half feet long, have wingspans exceeding four feet, and can weigh up to five pounds. Swooping down with clawed feet forward, they strike with such force that they can instantly kill prey larger than themselves. Great Horned Owls often smell of the skunks they have attacked, attesting to their fearlessness. They are identified by their "ear" tufts, white bibs, and huge yellow eyes. Their muffled *who-hoo-hoo-hooo* can be heard the year around, but especially during wintertime courtship. Great Horned Owls do not build nests. Instead, they use prior nests of large birds such as hawks and herons, or lay eggs in such places as barn lofts. Their eggs are white, nearly spherical, and typically number two or three per clutch. Nesting commences the earliest of any of our native birds, in January and February, so that nestlings are growing and fledge in April and May in synchrony with the emergence of the spring's first crop of young field mice and rabbits.

At 17 inches in length and with a wingspan of three feet, American Crows are the Midwest's largest "songbird" with the exception of the Common Raven (*Corvus corax*). They are numerous throughout the country and in a variety of habitats. They eat a variety of plant and animal material, and can even become predacious when the opportunity arises. Though typically noisy, crows can become mysteriously secretive around nests, which are usually hidden in pines or other concealing trees. Construction of stick nests commences in March. Four to five greenish-blue, speckled eggs hatch in 18 days, and the young fledge at around 35 days of age. Crows are migratory, but wintering flocks are found as far north as Canada. Increasingly, they are becoming common in urban areas. Renowned for their intelligence, crows are highly social. They often gang up on birds that they consider threats such as hawks, eagles, and especially, owls. At a disadvantage during the day, Great Horned Owls are often driven about amid the angry cawing of mobbing crows. Rarely, an owl will reach out with its foot and nab a crow that approaches too closely.

Great Horned Owl   American Crow

57

IDENTIFICATION TIPS

▶ large; gray-brown; puffy-headed
▶ large, moist brown eyes
▶ chest is barred; belly is streaked lengthwise
▶ white spots on back
▶ other owls, except Barn Owl, have yellow eyes

BARRED OWL

Strix varia

ike other nocturnal birds, Barred Owls are best detected by sound. Fortunately for identifiers, Barred Owls deliver one of the most recognizable of calls. It is a series of hoots with a distinctive rhythm, often rendered as *"who cooks for you . . . who cooks for you all."* The "all" ("aw") at the end of the call is characteristic. Barred Owls may be heard during any night of year and occasionally during daylight as well. Both males and females hoot and, when in full concert, will emit wild *yawls* and *chuckles*. Although one of our larger owls, Barred owls are not quite as large as Great Horned Owls. They average 17 inches in length and have wingspans of about 44 inches. Unlike Great Horneds, Barred Owls have no "ear" tufts, resulting in a rounded head. Additionally, they have dark rather than yellow eyes, and their plumage is barred.

Barred Owls are permanent residents throughout the eastern half of North America. Though absent from the mountainous and arid west, they range westward across Canada to the Rockies. This owl is most associated with forested bottomlands, especially where trees are huge. Their feet are small as compared to a Great Horned Owl's, being more suited to small prey such as voles, mice, and shrews. Because of their proximity to rivers, they also eat frogs, snakes, and crayfish.

Female Barred Owls lay two to three roundish, white eggs directly on the bottom of a hollow in a large broken or decaying tree. A pair may use the same nest site for many years in succession. The eggs hatch in 28 to 33 days. As is typical of owls, young leave the nest at a few weeks of age, well before they can fly. These flightless owlets are called "branchers" and, as they grow and test their wings, they will ultimately flutter to the ground. Well-meaning people sometimes pick them up, believing them to be abandoned. In reality, their parents will find and feed them nightly for several more weeks, often until they are beyond four months of age, when they are able to hunt on their own.

IDENTIFICATION TIPS

▶ slim-winged; gray-brown; often seen high in the air

▶ flies with easy strokes, changing quickly to quicker erratic strokes

▶ broad white bar across the long, pointed wings

▶ male has a white bar across its notched tail and a white throat

COMMON NIGHTHAWK

Chordeiles minor

ommon Nighthawks are nine inches long with two foot wingspans, and are often seen over towns near dusk. When illuminated by city lights from below, a white bar can be seen on each of their long, swept-back, pointed wings. Where one nighthawk is seen, there most certainly will be others, swooping low then climbing skyward again while repeatedly emitting *peent* calls.

They are also called "bullbats," and this fanciful name is little more misleading than "nighthawk," as they are seldom active after dark and are not hawks at all. Instead, they are members of a group known as *goatsuckers*, a name that also has a peculiar origin. An ancient myth, promulgated by Aristotle, maintained that a European relative of the Common Nighthawk used its wide mouth to suck milk from goats. In reality, the unusually broad mouths of the birds of this group are used to capture large flying insects, such as june bugs, cicadas, and moths.

These aerial insectivores become conspicuous over our cities with the return of warm, humid weather in early May. Not only are they benefited by the street lights that concentrate their prey, but the flat gravel roofs of downtown buildings offer a nesting alternative to the gravelly, barren areas that they used historically. Males court females by repeatedly diving from as high as 80 feet before flaring their wings and tail to produce a loud, low *boom*, usually over a prospective nest site. Perceived threats, such as humans who approach nests too closely, are sometimes startled by these diving birds. A person who has had a Common Nighthawk *boom* near his head, will long remember the event.

Common Nighthawks nest only once each season, usually beginning in May. Their two eggs are heavily speckled with brown. They hatch in 18 days. Roof-top nests can become dangerously hot for both eggs and young. Although fed by their parents, the young are able to move about somewhat to locate bits of shade during summer days and to escape other dangers. Chicks are able to fly at 18 days of age.

Common Nighthawks nest throughout most of North America. In August and September, hundreds can sometimes be seen migrating overhead during the daylight hours toward their winter home in South America.

IDENTIFICATION TIPS

▶ like all goatsuckers, they have large flat heads, small bills, and enormous mouths

▶ rounded wings

▶ male has large white tail patches and a white throat band; in females, these areas are buff-colored

▶ accent is on the first and last syllables of *whip-poor-will* call

▶ seen only at dusk unless flushed

WHIP-POOR-WILL
Caprimulgus vociferus

he strange name of this nocturnal bird is a verbal rendition of its call. This three-syllable whistle emanates from wooded areas, beginning in April. Just as daytime birds are most vocal at dawn and dusk, Whip-poor-wills sing most at the onset and conclusion of their period of activity, during the twilight minutes before dawn and after sunset. They often whistle all night, especially during a full moon, delivering hundreds of *whip-poor-wills* in quick succession. When this happens near homes, they are sometimes threatened by disturbed sleepers; however, most people are quick to defend what they consider to be a symbol of the wilderness that surrounds them.

These nine-inch-long birds have broad mouths for catching moths, june bugs, and cicadas. Unlike their Common Nighthawk "cousins," Whip-poor-wills seldom fly where they can be seen. Night travelers of rural gravel roads may see them sitting like chunks of wood on the roadway, their eyes glowing red in the headlights. Occasionally they are noticed during the day, resting longitudinally on horizontal limbs, in an attempt to blend in as part of the branch.

If during May and June they are flushed into flight from the forest floor, there is probably a nest nearby. Whip-poor-wills assemble no nesting material. They simply lay their two white, gray-mottled eggs directly on dry leaves. The eggs hatch in 19 days. Young are covered with silky down and are somewhat precocial, being able to shuffle about soon after hatching. A few weeks later, they are capable of their first flight.

Whip-poor-wills breed from the East Coast to Nebraska and Kansas. They nest only once a season. Calling subsides during mid-summer, when most young are being reared, but resumes briefly before their departure south in September. They winter along the Gulf Coast and through Central America.

IDENTIFICATION TIPS
- ▶ blackish swallowlike bird with long, slightly curved, stiff wings
- ▶ tail is stiff, slightly rounded, and never forked or fanned
- ▶ appears to beat its wings alternately rather than in unison; the effect is bat-like
- ▶ hold wings bowed in a crescent
- ▶ noisy chatter of chipping notes generally signifies Chimney Swifts are overhead

CHIMNEY SWIFT

Chaetura pelagica

Despite their familiarity in towns and cities across eastern North America, Chimney Swifts remain one of our bird curiosities. These sooty-gray birds are invariably seen in flight, their cylindrical, five-inch bodies propelled rapidly on slender, stiff wings. It has been suggested that they resemble "flying cigars." People sometimes mistake them for bats. They often course this way and that in little squadrons of two or three, chattering noisily, just above rooftops.

Chimney Swifts spend more time aloft than any other land bird, consuming flying insects, drinking, bathing, courting, and even copulating while on the wing. They are seldom seen perched, as this occurs only within an enclosure, commonly a chimney. Here they cling by their otherwise little-used toes while propping themselves up vertically with stiff tails.

April marks the return of these long distance migrants. Nesting commences in May. Their nests are composed of small, dead twigs that they snap from the tips of branches while in flight. These are fastened together forming a half-saucer on the inside of the chimney with a glue formed by the bird's own saliva. It is this saliva, from a different swift, that is used to make "bird's nest soup" in the Orient. Several Chimney Swift nests may be built in a single chimney, depending on its size. Each nest holds three to six white eggs. They hatch in 18 to 21 days. Fledglings that are unable to fly well sometimes fall into fireplaces.

Chimney Swifts assemble into flocks of thousands between the completion of their nesting season, in August, and their departure, in October. At dusk, these birds swirl about their favorite chimneys in hordes, passing over the top again and again before fluttering in to roost for the night. Over 10,000 were once counted entering a single industrial stack in Pennsylvania. After years of uncertainty, the Chimney Swift wintering ground was located when a Peruvian Indian was discovered wearing a necklace strung with the tiny leg bands put on nestlings by researchers in North America.

IDENTIFICATION TIPS

► male has glowing, fiery-red throat; iridescent green back

► female lacks red throat; tail tipped with white spots

RUBY-THROATED HUMMINGBIRD

Archilochus colubris

The smallest of the Midwest's birds is a mere three inches in length and weighs little more than a penny. Males have throats that gleam crimson in certain angles of light. Females have white throats with fine, dark speckles and white corners on their tails. Juveniles are colored like females except that the throats of those approaching a year of age are speckled with red.

These amazingly tiny, warm-blooded creatures require considerable amounts of high-energy foods to support their rapid metabolism. Hummingbirds fulfill this requirement with the carbohydrate-rich nectar that they obtain by hovering in place and probing their bills into a flower's center. When hovering, they stroke their wings over 50 times a second, producing a low humming sound as they maneuver forward, backward, sideways, and up and down. Favored flowers are tubular, and red to orange in color, including jewelweed, trumpet creeper, snapdragons, and columbine.

Hummingbirds serve as pollinators when moving from flower to flower. They appear to remember which flowers they have visited most recently and will not return to it until its nectar has been replenished. In addition to nectar, Ruby-throated Hummingbirds eat tiny insects, spiders, and larvae that they find in flowers, and they catch insects such as gnats in mid-air. Seemingly fearless, these exciting birds can be easily attracted with hummingbird feeders. Quarrels at feeders result in darting chases exceeding 30 miles per hour, during which wings whine and the birds squeak and twitter.

Ruby-throated Hummingbirds are the only regularly expected hummingbirds in the eastern half of the United States. They return to the Midwest to nest in late April and early May. Nests are made of lichens and spider web strands and usually situated high in trees, often over streams or lake shores. They are nearly impossible to find as they are saddled on a limb, only two inches across and camouflaged with bits of lichen. Their two white eggs are no bigger than peanuts. The young hatch in two weeks and fly from the nest three weeks later. This species nests twice a summer.

Late summer numbers are bolstered by the addition of the new young, which resemble females. By late September, most Ruby-throats have departed for Mexico and Central America. Some cross the Gulf of Mexico in a single, 500-mile flight.

IDENTIFICATION TIPS

▶ perched, it is big-headed and big-billed; larger than a Robin

▶ blue-gray above, with a ragged bushy crest and a broad gray breast band

▶ female has an additional rusty breast band

▶ hovers on rapidly-beating wings before diving

▶ seen singly or in pairs along streams and ponds

▶ has deep, irregular wingbeats in flight

▶ loud rattling call

▶ except for terns, kingfishers are the only small birds that dive headfirst into water

BELTED KINGFISHER

Ceryle alcyon

These heavily-built, foot-long birds perch in the open along streams and lake shores. They are easily recognized by their large, crested heads, bluish-gray upper-parts, and their white bellies with the blue chest-bands that give them their name. Females have an additional belt of brown. In flight, they emit a loud, rattling call. Their wing-beats are deep and irregular.

Belted Kingfishers prefer clear water so that they can spy fish swimming just beneath the surface. They sometimes hover at heights of up to 30 feet before dropping bill first into the water. Often it is the splash that first attracts a person's attention. Catches are usually small fish that are carried to a perch in the bill. Holding the fish by the tail, the bird swings its head repeatedly against the perch, stunning it before swallowing it headfirst.

Belted Kingfishers range across North America. They migrate south in winter to areas of open water and back north in spring, nesting in all but the hottest and driest regions of the country. Nests are excavated in vertical banks of soil, usually in riverbanks. Burrow entrances can sometimes be spotted by boaters. They are two to three feet below the top of the bank, four inches in diameter, and have two tracks at the bottom resulting from the bird's feet. A tunnel extends upward from the entrance for a short distance and then back into the bank as far as ten feet before terminating in a spherical egg chamber about 12-inches in diameter.

Here the female lays her four to five white eggs, in April or May. They hatch following 22 to 24 days of incubation and the young depart the burrow about a month later. Belted Kingfishers nest once a year.

IDENTIFICATION TIPS
▶ entirely red head
▶ solid black back, white rump
▶ large square white wing patches are conspicuous (making the lower back look white when the bird is at rest)
▶ sexes similar
▶ immature is dusky-headed; large white wing patch identifies it

♂

♀

RED-HEADED WOODPECKER
Melanerpes erythrocephalus

Because of their easily-recognized, spectacular coloration, these nine-inch woodpeckers are favorites throughout their eastern United States range. Their popularity persists despite their tendency to periodically vanish for months or even years at a time. It is not unusual for an ornithologist to be asked: "What has become of Red-headed Woodpeckers?"

In reality, Red-headed numbers simply fluctuate from place to place in response to nest site and food availability. In spring, they concentrate where nesting habitat is abundant, such as farm groves with decaying trees and the flooded dead timber in the backwaters of reservoirs. Though they do not make regular migrations like other birds, in fall they are capable of traversing several states to locate a good crop of small acorns, a favored food. In addition to acorns, they eat berries, grains, vegetables, tree sap, and insects. The latter are drilled for in trees, picked from the ground, and even caught in mid-air. Red-headeds are sometimes attracted to bird feeders offering sunflower seeds and suet.

Red-headed Woodpeckers' loud, rather grating, *kweer* cries are most prevalent during March and April as they pair up for the breeding season. Both members of the pair, which look alike, excavate the nesting cavity during April and May, usually in the open, well up on a dead tree. Entrances are about two inches in diameter. The nesting chamber extends as far as two feet down the center of the trunk. Females commonly lay five eggs on a cushion of wood chips. She and her mate exchange incubation duties. The eggs hatch at around two weeks and the young leave the nest about three weeks later. Occasionally, the pair will nest a second time in a season.

Newly fledged young are streaked with brown except for white wing patches. As they molt into adult plumage, their heads turn red last, and brown-headed juveniles can be recognized even into their second year.

IDENTIFICATION TIPS

▶ black and white "ladder" barring on back; red cap and white rump

▶ red covers crown and nape in male, but only nape in female

▶ juvenile is also ladder-backed, but has a brown head that shows no red

RED-BELLIED WOODPECKER

Melanerpes carolinus

These nine-inch woodpeckers are well known, except from the northern and western portions of the Midwest where they do not live. Within their range, which extends from Kansas to the East Coast, they are birds of the woodland edge and commonly visit suburban and rural yards. They can easily be enticed to bird feeders stocked with sunflower seeds. They have black-and-white cross-barring on their backs, and red caps. The red extends completely over the top of a male's head, whereas the top of a female's head is gray. The name "Red-bellied" is mystifying unless a bird is examined closely. Though there is a rose wash on the tummy, it seems inconceivable that those who named this species could not come up with a better name.

Because Red-bellied Woodpeckers are able to drill wood-boring beetles and larvae from wood in winter as well as summer, they are nonmigratory throughout most of their range. In addition, they eat various nuts, fruits, and seeds, especially from fall through spring. As a result, they are easily attracted to bird feeders. Perhaps because of their threatening bill, other feeder birds give them a wide berth, and they are usually free to sit and eat their fill.

The Red-bellied Woodpecker's most familiar call, which can be heard at any season, is a trilling *churr*. Beginning in spring, especially in response to nearby members of the opposite sex, both males and females emit *ta-wik - ta-wik - ta-wik* calls. Loud drumming, which is another courtship sound, is delivered in bursts lasting about one second.

From April through July, Red-bellied Woodpeckers excavate holes measuring about two inches in diameter in the decayed tops of trees. Cavities are about one foot deep. Like most eggs sheltered in darkness, the eggs require no concealing coloration, so they are white. The four to five eggs hatch in 11 days, and the young leave the cavity 24 to 26 days later. Red-bellied Woodpeckers raise two broods in the south and one in the north.

As typical of woodpeckers, Red-bellieds excavate a new cavity with each nesting. This is important ecologically as old cavities secondarily provide habitat for a variety of cavity-nesting wildlife, ranging from bluebirds to chickadees to flying squirrels.

IDENTIFICATION TIPS

▶ white back; small, slender bill

▶ small edition of the Hairy Woodpecker, which
  is larger and has a large bill

▶ barred outer tail feathers are diagnostic

DOWNY WOODPECKER

Picoides pubescens

These common, six-inch woodpeckers are tiny compared to their relatives. Black and white, like most woodpeckers, their only brilliance is a spot of red at the back of the head present in males only. They are nearly identical to Hairy Woodpeckers (*Picoides villosus*), who likewise are distributed nearly throughout the North American continent. Hairy Woodpeckers, however, are less common, nearly two inches longer, have bills nearly as long as their heads, and their white outer tail feathers are pure white. Downy Woodpeckers have bills much shorter than their heads, and their white tail feathers are flecked with black. The two species even sound similar, emitting a single *pik* or a long, descending rattle.

Downy Woodpeckers can be seen at any time of year in suburban yards, mixed woodlands, and even cultivated areas. Their size enables them to work small twigs and stems that are out of the reach of their larger relatives. They consume wood-boring beetles, larvae, ants, and in the fall, can be seen extracting borers from corn stalks or hammering apart an insect gall on a goldenrod stem. They also visit feeding stations for seeds and suet.

Courtship drumming and pairing commence in late winter but actual nesting does not usually get underway until May. Nesting cavities are excavated in the dead parts of trees, frequently just beneath a broken-off top. The parents take turns incubating the four to six pure white eggs. Incubation requires 12 days, and the young fly form the nest cavity at 20 to 23 days of age. Their parents feed them for another two weeks before initiating a second nesting.

Like other woodpeckers, Downy Woodpeckers have a long, barbed tongue for extracting insects from deep in wood. It can project the length of the bill beyond the bill-tip. For the necessary elasticity, a woodpecker's tongue extends through the back of the skull, beneath the skin over the top of the head, and is anchored near a nostril.

IDENTIFICATION TIPS

▶ jay sized with brown back, no white on the wings, and a black breast crescent

▶ in flight, the white rump is conspicuous; yellow under wings and tail

▶ often hop awkwardly on the ground; flight is deeply undulating

NORTHERN FLICKER

Colaptes auratus

 hese large, common woodpeckers often eat ants on or near the ground. Especially during their spring and fall migrations, when one is seen, there are likely others scattered about the lawn or forest floor. They are 11 inches long and the only North American woodpeckers to be primarily brown rather than black and white. They have white rumps, black bibs, and spotted breasts. Those that live from the Great Plains to the East Coast have wing and tail feathers with vivid yellow patterns. This contributes to a yellow underwing that can be seen in flight. The identifiable yellow-shafted feathers are sometimes noticed on the ground during the late-summer molt.

Typical of woodpeckers in flight, Northern Flickers alternate between flapping and tucking their wings, resulting in an undulating, roller-coaster flight. Their call is a prolonged *wicka . . . wicka . . . wicka*, primarily given as the birds are pairing-up in spring. A courting pair performs a dance involving the spreading of wings and tail while emitting a slow *cha . . . weeka . . . cha . . . weeka* in unison. Males have black "moustaches" at the corner of their bills, whereas females have none. The male is the primary excavator of the nesting cavity, typically in the trunks of dead trees. Entrances are roundish, about three-and-a-half inches in diameter, and most often face to the east or south. The nest chamber continues down into the tree trunk another foot. It is lined with wood chips for the six to eight white eggs. The eggs hatch in 11 days and the young exit the nest cavity 24 to 27 days later.

In addition to ants, Northern Flickers eat a variety of insects that they chisel from trees, as well as berries and seeds. They sometimes visit bird feeding stations for sunflower seeds and suet. Though Northern Flickers migrate short distances, they live year-round across most of the United States.

IDENTIFICATION TIPS

▶ great size; solid black back; flaming red crest
▶ sweeping wingbeats and flashing white under wing areas identify the Pileated in flight
▶ large oval or oblong holes in dead trees indicate its presence
▶ call is a series, never single

PILEATED WOODPECKER

Dryocopus pileatus

With the disappearance of Ivory-billed Woodpeckers (*Campephilus principalis*), these are the largest and most dramatic woodpeckers remaining in North America. At 15 inches in length, they are nearly as large as crows. The diagnostic flaming red crest is present on both sexes, but the male of the pair is identified by a red "moustache" whereas the female's is black. Additionally, the female has a black forehead. When flying overhead, they sail directly and with seeming effortlessness, their broad wings nearly closing with each deep stroke. Their loud, rapid *wuk wuk wuk wuk* call rings through the woods at any season and has such a wild quality as to be used as recorded background sounds in jungle movies. It has been described as a laugh and, although the cartoon version of their sound is rather inaccurate, these birds were the model for "Woody the Woodpecker."

Many people erroneously believe these birds to be rare or even endangered. But those who live near or visit large bottomland forests have opportunities to encounter them. Pileated Woodpeckers rarely stray from the deep woods and are especially associated with the huge trees of river floodplains. Although they range through forested landscapes from the East Coast westward through Missouri and the Great Lakes states, they are essentially absent from sparingly forested, highly cultivated regions, including much of Illinois, Indiana, Ohio, and almost all of Iowa. Though missing from the Great Plains through the arid west, they take up residence again in the Pacific Northwest and live throughout the boreal forests of Canada. Where they do reside they are year-round residents.

These impressive woodpeckers eat mostly wood boring beetles and larvae. Using their heavy, three-inch bill to alternately hammer, pry, and rip, whole portions of a rotting tree can be splintered apart in a matter of seconds. The underlying morsels are nabbed up with a tongue that projects well beyond the bill. They also eat grains and nuts. Pileated Woodpeckers can sometimes be attracted to feeding stations that offer suet.

These large woodpeckers pair for life. Nesting cavities are excavated in trunks of large trees in spring. The oval entrance is about three inches wide by four inches high. By May, the parents are exchanging incubation duties. There is an average of four white eggs. They hatch in 18 days. The young leave the nest cavity about a month later.

IDENTIFICATION TIPS

▶ sparrow-sized
▶ similar to the Eastern Phoebe, but with 2 narrow white wing bars and a light lower beak
▶ lack of contrast between head and back
▶ no eye ring
▶ usually do not wag their tails
▶ immature Eastern Phoebes have buffy wing bars in fall, but their breasts are lemon yellow

EASTERN WOOD-PEWEE

Contopus virens

astern Wood-Pewees are rather small, nondescript flycatchers that are more often heard than seen. They live in deciduous forests in the eastern half of North America. Named for their song, they emit a high, thin *pee-ah-wee* that wafts through the woods on late spring and summer days. Through diligence, the singer can usually be sighted, typically perched on a bare limb in the forest mid-story. Their relatively large, crowned heads identify them as flycatchers. Eastern Wood-Pewees are five-and-a-quarter inches in length and are dark gray above and lighter gray below. The presence of wing-bars distinguishes them from Eastern Phoebes

Eastern Wood-Pewees are one of the latest migrants to return in spring, having traveled from South America. Their appearance in May coincides with a major emergence of flying insects. Like other flycatchers, Eastern Wood-Pewees take insects during short flights, returning to the same perch again and again. Their cup nests are built well out on the upper surface of a horizontal branch and covered with lichens until indistinguishable from knots. The Eastern Wood-Pewee's eggs are white with wreaths of purple spots. There are two to five eggs in a clutch. They hatch after 13 days of incubation. It may require another two weeks for the young to depart the nest. Despite the Eastern Wood-Pewee's abundance, little else is known of their reproductive behavior, including whether or not they nest more than once a season.

IDENTIFICATION TIPS

▶ tail-bobbing is diagnostic

▶ solid black bill

▶ gray-brown; sparrow-sized; dark head (darker than back; head of Eastern Wood-Pewee is same shade as back)

▶ no eye ring or strong wing bars

▶ immatures can be mistaken for pewees because of their dull wing bars

EASTERN PHOEBE

Sayornis phoebe

lthough simply small, dark birds, Eastern Phoebes attract attention. Foremost, they tend to live near people, especially in rural areas, nesting on porches, in out-buildings, and under eaves, decks, and docks. At six inches in length, they are dark gray above and light below. Like other members of the fly-catcher family, they have the hint of a crest on their head, but unlike most flycatchers, they lack wing-bars, except for first-year birds. The best identifiers are the manner in which they continually bob their tail up and down, and their raspy, atonal *fee-bee* calls. This sound can be heard immediately upon the Phoebe's return in March and continues through much of the summer.

Eastern Phoebes are remarkably solitary. Although monogamous, seldom is more than one seen at the same time, even when nesting. The female alone con-structs the nest where it will be sheltered from above, often along streams, under rock ledges and bridges, but also on buildings. The four-inch wide by four-inch high nest is composed of varying amounts of mud, depending on the need for it to adhere to a surface. It is covered with moss and lined with fine grasses, feath-ers, and hair. It may take a week or two for a nest to be completed and then it may sit empty for another week before receiving its first egg, usually in early April. Typical clutches contain five eggs. The eggs are milky white. They hatch in 16 days. The young fledge 16 days later.

The parents fall silent while nesting, but as their youngsters fledge, the adults resume calling in preparation for another nesting. Previous nests are renovated or new nests constructed for the second and final family of the year. These young typically take flight in July. Following a late summer molt, Eastern Phoebes depart in September for their winter range. Eastern Phoebes nest from the East Coast to the Great Plains, and winter from the southern states through northern Mexico.

IDENTIFICATION TIPS

▶ broad bill; large head; rusty wings and tail; gray chest; yellow belly

▶ no other eastern flycatcher has a long rust-colored tail

▶ often erects a bushy crest

GREAT CRESTED FLYCATCHER

Myiarchus crinitus

Usually the first clue that a Great Crested Flycatcher is around is the loud, ascending *wheeeeep* call coming from the tree tops. This noisy flycatcher is still hard to pick out among the foliage. Its yellow underside is often glimpsed first, and then the rusty color of the wings and tail as it flits among the branches. More careful observation will discern the gray throat and breast, and the flycatcher family's trademark crown.

Although only seven inches long, Great Crested Flycatchers are the largest and most observable of our woodland flycatchers, inhabiting woodland edges and the scattered trees of parks, pastures, and suburban yards. They glean bugs and worms from leaves, and make short flights to take moths and flies from the air. Wintering from Mexico to Venezuela, they finally return to nest in May, just when the tender, new leaves begin to support high numbers of insects.

Cavity nesters, they typically choose holes produced when branches have broken off of dead trees. Occasionally they use man-made structures such as mailboxes and birdhouses. Their relatively large clutches of up to eight eggs hatch in about 15 days. The young fledge in another 15 days. They nest once and are on their way south by the end of August.

Great Crested Flycatchers often locate shed snake skins to place in their nesting cavities, together with their nesting material. This may deter cavity nesting competitors and predators who recognize snakes as threats. Cavities containing snake skins tend to be avoided by mice and flying squirrels, known predators of eggs and nestlings.

IDENTIFICATION TIPS

▶ complete, broad, white band across the tail tip is diagnostic

▶ a concealed red crown is rarely seen

▶ waxwings often act like flycatchers, but they have a yellow tail band

EASTERN KINGBIRD

Tyrannus tyrannus

hese open-country flycatchers are most likely seen perched on fence wires or utility lines along rural roads. At eight inches in length, they are immaculate white below and dark charcoal above. The best identifier is a white band completely across the tip of the tail, present in no other North American songbird. Their heads are slightly crested, as is characteristic of members of the flycatcher family. The narrow red streak down the middle of the crown is seldom noticed. Their call is an emphatic *bzzzzt*.

As is typical of flycatchers, Eastern Kingbirds make short, sallying flights from perches as they catch flying insects. Bees constitute their diet to the degree that in some locations, they are known as "bee martins." Their common name, "kingbird," stems from their commanding relationship with other birds. Acting individually or as pairs, they fearlessly drive birds as large as hawks from their premises with repeated dives and actual physical contact. Their Latin name, *Tyrannus*, meaning "tyrant," also originates from this domineering manner.

Eastern Kingbirds breed from the East Coast west to a line from Texas to British Columbia. Having wintered in South America, they arrive back on their breeding grounds in late April and early May. Pairing ensues and nest building commences in June. Although nesting areas are typically open fields, Eastern Kingbirds require a few trees in which to build their nests. Most nests are situated well out on a limb and so bulky that they can quite easily be seen when looking up through the branches. The two to five white, brown-spotted eggs hatch in 15 days, and the young fledge 17 days later, usually in early July. They nest only once a season. Their relatively low reproductive rate is countered by prolonged parental care following fledging, which improves the survival of young.

IDENTIFICATION TIPS

▶ blue-gray cap contrasts with olive back
▶ strong, white eyebrow stripe is bordered by black
▶ red iris is not obvious at a distance
▶ song repeated as often as 40 times per minute, and typically continues for many minutes without a long break

RED-EYED VIREO
Vireo olivaceus

These are North America's most vocal birds. Their song is robin-like except divided by short pauses into sweet, clear phrases resembling *cheeree..cheeryup..cheerwit*. It can be heard from within almost any substantial woods between April and July from the break of day through the heat of the afternoon. A single individual is reported to have sung an amazing 22,197 times within a ten-hour period.

Despite nearly everyone having heard these common forest birds at one time or another, few have taken the time to pick out their song from among the various melodies emanating from the woods. Red-eyed Vireos are not as lively as wood warblers; people who make the effort are often able to study an individual with binoculars as it hunts through the foliage. In addition to their surprisingly red eyes, these five-and-a-half inch olive songbirds have a white and black strip above the eye. They are otherwise rather plain and lack wing-bars. The sexes are alike. Those younger than a year have dark rather than red irises.

Vireos, in general, have relatively heavy bills that have tiny hooks at the tip for picking caterpillars and crawling insects from leaves and twigs. Having wintered in the Amazon Basin, Red-eyed Vireos return to their North American range in April. Their arrival coincides with the emergence of new, succulent leaves, which are especially inviting to their insect prey. They weave nests of grasses and fibers that hang from their brims in the forks of lateral branches. In this way, their nests are similar to those of orioles, but shallower.

Red-eyed Vireos typically lay a clutch of four eggs. They usually raise two families a year, beginning in May and ending in July. No bird species is more heavily parasitized by Brown-headed Cowbirds. Despite this handicap, Red-eyed Vireos remain common residents of our deciduous forests.

IDENTIFICATION TIPS

▶ showy blue bird with a crest; larger than a robin
▶ bold white spots in the wings and tail; whitish/dull-gray underparts
▶ black necklace
▶ rather noisy

BLUE JAY

Cyanocitta cristata

 onspicuous and fascinating to watch, Blue Jays exhibit many of the characteristics of their crow relatives. Nearly everyone from throughout the Midwest and eastward knows these common, ten-inch-long birds. People who feed birds often get the chance to witness their sociality. A few bird watchers disapprove of the Blue Jay's gang-like aggressiveness and their opinion of them is further reduced when they learn that Blue Jays tend to prey on the eggs and nestlings of other birds. The Blue Jays, of course, are only behaving as designed by the forces of natural selection, and it is unfair to evaluate them with human standards.

Members of the crow family, in general, are renowned for their intelligence, and the Blue Jay's large vocal repertoire provides a hint of their surprising intellect. It has been suggested that they communicate with as many as 21 different sounds, each with a distinct meaning. Included in this "language" is the commonly heard *jay* call, which gives them their name. It is reminiscent of a jeer and, fittingly, is used to muster Blue Jays in the mobbing of perceived threats. "Pumphandle" or "bell" calls are accompanied by the pumping of the body and function to alert the others. Females greet other females with "rattle" calls as they assemble in trees. Jays also emit peeps, clucks, and "whisper songs," delivered when in close proximity to each other, thus resembling conversation.

Blue Jays migrate in fall to where foods such as acorns are available. Despite this movement, they reside in most of their summer range throughout the year. Monogamous, with sexes identical, pairs become silent when near their nests, which are well-hidden in trees. Nests are made of sticks and are about nine inches across. Clutches are laid in April and May. They usually contain four to five eggs, which are greenish-buff and speckled. The female incubates the eggs and they hatch in 17 to 18 days. The young leave the nest at around 17 days of age, before fully capable of flight.

Blue Jays are omnivorous, eating a wide variety of animal and plant material. This trait, plus their remarkable intelligence, has allowed them to thrive despite environmental changes caused by humans. Blue Jays that visit bird feeders often arrive as a group and behave warily. They may swallow as many as 20 sunflower seeds whole before flying to a safe location to spit them out. They then crack them open one by one while holding them under their toes.

IDENTIFICATION TIPS

- ▶ brown ground bird; larger than a sparrow
- ▶ black breast mark and facial design identify it
- ▶ walks; doesn't hop
- ▶ when overhead, the bird looks pale with a black tail; folds wings after each beat
- ▶ female and immature are duller, but with the same basic pattern

HORNED LARK

Eremophila alpestris

**O**f the nearly 80 larks in the world, there is only one native to North America, the exquisitely-marked Horned Lark of our open countryside. Horned Larks nest throughout North America and well up into the Arctic Circle. They vacate their northern range in fall, retreating to the lower 48 states. Here they assemble into wintering flocks of a few dozen to a few hundred individuals, avoiding trees and favoring flat terrain with short, sparse vegetation.

These six-and-a-half-inch songbirds walk rather than hop as they forage for seeds, commonly in grain stubble and plowed fields. They typically fly as a group lowly and slowly for a short distance across the field. Their white outer tail feathers show as they land. During snowstorms, they sometimes gather along highways and in feedlots. During cold weather they become so preoccupied with feeding that they can be approached closely enough to see that they are more than simply little brown birds. They are marked with yellow and black on the face and neck. They derive their name from the tufts on either side of their crown.

Although most noticed during the winter, some Horned Larks remain with us to nest. Nesting habitat includes airports, golf courses, grazed pastures and fallow crop fields. They are the earliest songbird to nest — their weak, tinkling courtship songs can be heard beginning in February. These singers are typically perched on only a slight rise, such as a clod of earth, well out in a field. Like the skylarks of Europe and Asia, Horned Larks sing when in flight. A courting male climbs skyward, then spreads his wings and tail to glide downward while delivering his jingling song. Before reaching the ground, he climbs and sings again and may continue his aerial display for several minutes. This courtship flight takes place over a chosen nesting area.

Females build nests of stems, grass, husks, or other crop residue in a shallow excavation and assemble objects such as pebbles, stones, and corn cobs to one side, perhaps to serve as windbreaks. She lays three to five eggs that are softly-splotched with tan on a gray background. They hatch in 11 days. Horned Larks can nest twice each season.

IDENTIFICATION TIPS

▶ male is uniformly blue-black all over (no other swallow is dark all over)

▶ female is light-bellied; throat and breast grayish, often with a faint collar above

▶ glides in circles; often spreads tail

▶ largest North American swallow

♀

♂

PURPLE MARTIN

Progne subis

These eight-inch swallows are named for the glossy, deep blue plumage of the males. Females and males younger than two years are brownish with light bellies and, if it were not for their larger size, might be confused with other swallows. Like other members of their family, Purple Martins catch insects from the air during extended flights. Unlike their smaller relatives, however, they tend to forage higher and on larger prey. Foods include airborne beetles, flies, moths, wasps, dragonflies, grasshoppers, and insects as large as cicadas.

Purple Martins are unique among birds in that throughout most of their range they nest only in homes provided specifically for them by humans. Once tree cavity nesters, they took to man-made quarters so readily that by 1900, they rarely nested in natural sites. Many people around the country invite colonies to their yards with specially-designed martin houses. The liquid twittering of Purple Martins perched along wires, and their graceful, sweeping flight overhead add a decorative feature to a neighborhood. Additionally, many Purple Martin landlords attest that their birds consume volumes of insect pests.

Males arrive on the breeding grounds in March, preceding females by a week to ten days. This is surprisingly early and potentially hazardous considering their dependency on flying insects. An early arrival is a worthwhile gamble, however, as it enables them to claim the most desirable nesting sites. Nesting begins in May. A clutch of four to five white eggs hatches in 15 days and the young fly a month later. Martins nest once a season in the northern part of their range and twice in the south. They breed from the East Coast through the Great Plains and sparingly through the Desert Southwest and along the West Coast.

After rearing of young is completed, in July, Purple Martins begin perching on power lines in neighborhoods as they prepare for their remarkable journey south. These flocks gradually coalesce with others until there may be immense flocks of thousands in only a few locales. By late August, they have vanished and are well on their way to their distant winter range. They winter east of the Andes in South America, often as huge flocks in cities such as Sao Paulo, Brazil.

IDENTIFICATION TIPS

▶ green-blue/black on back, clear white below

▶ glides in circles; ends each glide with 3 or 4 quick flaps and a short climb

▶ immature has dusky brown back and incomplete breastband; easy to confuse with Rough-winged Swallow (it has a dingier throat), or Bank Swallow (it has a complete breast band); Tree Swallow's throat is always white

TREE SWALLOW

Tachycineta bicolor

These five-inch-long swallows gleam with metallic greens and blues depending on the angle of light. They are immaculate white below and their tails are shallowly forked. Where one is seen, there are usually several, each darting and swooping independently after airborne insects over ponds and meadows. Though most swallow species shun trees to an extent, Tree Swallows readily perch in them, befitting their name. They also nest in tree cavities, especially in dead trees near water that have been hollowed out by woodpeckers.

Tree Swallows breed across North America with the exception of the deep south, the arid west, and the treeless tundra of the far north. Generally, they are most numerous in cooler, damper climates. They return from Mexico and Central America to various latitudes of their breeding range between late March and early May. Their arrival proceeds egg laying by several weeks because, as with Purple Martins, an early return is an advantage in competing for appropriate nesting sites. Perhaps because of nest cavity competition, Tree Swallows often use man-made nest boxes, occasionally occupying those intended for bluebirds.

Tree Swallows construct a cup of fine grasses at the base of the cavity and then proceed to line it with downy feathers that they find scattered about. Males collect the nest material and are sometimes so desperate for feathers that they swoop close by to catch those that people toss into the air for them. Over 100 feathers have been counted in a single nest. The female assembles the material and alone incubates the four to six glossy white eggs for the two week incubation period. Both parents feed the young for 15 to 25 days while in the nest. As the young near their fledging date, the parents must work feverishly to keep them fed.

Young Tree Swallows can be seen flying with adults as early as June. They are brown in place of green until the following spring, and are difficult to distinguish from other swallows. Tree Swallows nest only once each year.

IDENTIFICATION TIPS

▶ brown back, brown throat and breast distinguish it from other birds
▶ no breast band
▶ in flight, the wings are pulled back at the end of each stroke

NORTHERN ROUGH-WINGED SWALLOW

Stelgidopteryx serripennis

hese are the quintessential little brown birds. There are few swallow-like birds so dully-colored except female and immature Purple Martins, which are substantially larger. At five-and-a-half inches in length, Northern Rough-winged Swallows are simply brown above with dusky throats and breasts grading to white on the belly. Although recognizable as swallows from their continuous flight and long, swept back wings, they are otherwise so indistinguishable as to be named for the rough texture of the outer primary quill.

Northern Rough-winged Swallows consume flying insects, typically over lakes, rivers, and meadows. They characteristically cruise swiftly within a foot or two of the grass or water's surface, then swoop upward to change direction before another low pass. Usually several will forage in the same area though not necessarily together. Feeding may continue for hours with the birds rarely taking time to land. When they do roost, it is usually with their own kind. They select thin, open perches such as the tips of bare branches or utility wires. Typical of swallows, their feet are designed for perching rather than walking.

Northern Rough-winged Swallows return from the tropics in early April and spread across the Lower 48 States. Nesting occurs where there are existing holes such as crevices in rock ledges or burrows in earthen banks. Highway travelers often see them flittering about the faces of road-cuts. Where several crevices occur together, Rough-winged Swallows will form small nesting colonies. Grass and stems are used to construct a cup for the clutch of four to six white eggs. They hatch in 16 days. The young wait until able to fly well before departing the nest, at around 20 days of age, in late June or early July. There is only one nesting each summer. Large flocks assemble in September when preparing for the fall migration.

IDENTIFICATION TIPS

▶ rusty orange rump, square tail, broad wings, buff-colored forehead

▶ overhead, the bird appears square-tailed, with a dark throat patch

▶ glides in a long eclipse, ending each glide with a steep climb

▶ soars more than other swallows

CLIFF SWALLOW

Petrochelidon pyrrhonota

ike other swallows, Cliff Swallows are readily seen because they feed on airborne flies out in the open. What makes them even more conspicuous, however, is the fact that there are so many of them. Because they are colonial, people tend to see none or many, but if a total tally of their numbers were possible, they might prove to be the most abundant bird species in North America. Their abundance is partly due to their huge breeding range, which extends from Alaska through all but the most arid regions of the west and nearly to the East Coast. Within this domain, they form large colonies, some containing as many as 3,500 nesting pairs.

These standard-sized swallows are about five inches in length and readily identified by their orange rumps, easily seen when in flight. Their tail is squared-off, rather than forked, and they have a spot of buff on the forehead. The sexes are alike. They emit a melodious, purring call as they fly about.

Though distributed widely today, up until the mid-1800s, Cliff Swallows were restricted to the mountainous west where they construct their unique, funnel-shaped, mud nests beneath rocky ledges. A lack of cliffs on the Great Plains prevented them from expanding their range into eastern North America until humans constructed bridges, a suitable substitute for cliffs, throughout the plains. Now that Cliff Swallows have bridged that gap, they have colonized much of the eastern half of the continent where they sometimes have reverted to nest on natural sites. After an initial boom, Cliff Swallows have declined since the mid-1900s, perhaps because of the removal of old barns, a common nest site, and competition with House Sparrows, who take over nests.

Throughout most of the eastern United States, Cliff Swallows nest primarily on manmade structures, including buildings, bridges, culverts, and dams. Colonies sometimes resemble numerous mud jugs packed closely together. The first and only brood is raised from May through July. Incubation of the two to six speckled eggs requires two weeks and rearing another two. In September, Cliff Swallows form huge flocks of many thousands in preparation for migration. They winter in South America.

IDENTIFICATION TIPS
▶ only swallow that is truly swallow-tailed (deeply forked)
▶ only swallow with white tail spots
▶ flight is direct and close to the ground; not much gliding
▶ other swallows with rusty underparts have orange rumps

BARN SWALLOW

Hirundo rustica

**B**arn Swallows are denizens of rural landscapes across North America. They are so associated with the countryside that their scientific name, *rustica*, means "of the country" in Latin. These sleek, six-inch swallows are exquisitely designed for continuous flight and high maneuverability because of their swept-back wings and deeply-forked tails. Where one is seen, there are typically others, cruising swiftly within a few feet of the ground over pastures or near herds of cattle, capturing the flying insects that compose their diet. Or they will sweep deftly into open barn doors or hover in place, often while twittering constantly.

Barn Swallows return in early April but do not usually begin nesting until May. Because their nests are made from mud, they must be situated where protected from rain. Barns, other open buildings, bridges, and porches are usual sites, especially if there is suitable mud in the vicinity at the time of construction. Both members of the pair carry beads of mud in their bills and plaster it to the side of a rafter or similar structure, forming a half-cup. The mud is strengthened with interwoven straw. Fine straw is used to line the nest, as are poultry feathers to warm and cushion the eggs. Nest construction can take a week.

Clutches contain four to six eggs, which are white with brown speckles. They require 14 days of incubation, and the young fly from the nest at 20 days of age. Where conditions are favorable, several pairs will nest together. As many as 50 nests have been reported in a single barn. Nests are reused to raise another brood, typically in July.

Following the nesting period, adults and new young perch along power lines near farmsteads throughout the countryside. As fall sets in, they coalesce into fewer but larger flocks, containing thousands. They migrate by day, beginning in September. The Barn Swallow's wintering range extends from Panama to the tip of South America. They also occur throughout Europe, Africa, and Asia, and are one of the world's most widespread birds.

IDENTIFICATION TIPS
▶ tiny; black cap and bib with white cheeks
▶ sides are buff-colored

BLACK-CAPPED CHICKADEE

Poecile atricapillus

These four-and-a-half inch packets of energy are among North America's best known birds. They are common wherever mature trees predominate, whether in cities or the country. Their song is a clear, two- to three-noted whistle with the first note the highest. They are permanent residents and singing can commence soon after the first of the year. Their scold is the sassy *chick-a-dee-dee* that gives them their name. Chickadees can easily be attracted to bird feeders with sunflower seeds and suet. Feeders designed to exclude large birds, such as mesh bags, are easily mastered by them because of their ability to land and cling on vertical surfaces or even upside down. They employ the same acrobatics to pick insects from branches and seeds from seed heads.

Black-capped Chickadees live from New England to Alaska, and from the limit of trees in the far north, southward to a line extending from mid-Missouri to mid-Ohio. At that point, their range abruptly ends and they are replaced by Carolina Chickadees (*Poecile carolinensis*). This species is nearly identical in appearance but has a song that is four-parted and up-down-up-down in tone. Carolina Chickadees inhabit most of the southeastern states.

Black-capped Chickadees excavate nesting cavities in rotting wood or use abandoned woodpecker holes and birdhouses. Nests are made of moss and plant fibers, and lined with hair and feathers. Only the female incubates the large clutch of five to ten white, speckled eggs. She is regularly fed by her mate during this two-week period. The young are fed by both parents during the two weeks that they are growing in the nest and up to a month after leaving the cavity. Nesting takes place from April through June. In some areas, a second nesting may follow the first.

Despite weighing only one-third ounce, Black-capped Chickadees are able to survive temperatures of minus 50 degrees Fahrenheit. To conserve energy during severe cold, they fluff their feathers, tuck up their legs, and lower their body temperature by up to 20 degrees.

IDENTIFICATION TIPS

▶ small, gray, mouse-colored; rust-colored flanks

▶ tufted crest

▶ usually found in flocks of 3-8 birds

TUFTED TITMOUSE

Baeolophus bicolor

hese five-and-a-half inch, gray, crested songbirds are residents of deciduous forests of the southeastern states, including the southern part of the Midwest. Their numbers decline northward through Missouri, Illinois, Indiana, and Ohio, and they are absent from most of Iowa, Wisconsin, and Michigan. Nevertheless, they are included in this book because where they do occur, they are one of the more familiar of birds.

People know Tufted Titmice primarily because they are one of the easiest birds to attract to bird feeders. In fact, there is some evidence that they are expanding their range northward because of the increasing popularity of this hobby. Like their relatives the chickadees, Tufted Titmice are able to cling and dangle from feeders to select preferred seeds. They especially favor sunflower seeds which they hold beneath their toes to hammer open with their bills. Those kernels not immediately swallowed are flown to nearby trees to be pressed between furrows of bark, presumably to be consumed later.

Tufted Titmice are permanent residents throughout their range. A pair may reside in the same few acres throughout life. Especially at the onset of the breeding season, from February through April, their loud *peter-peter-peter* calls echo through the woodland from every direction. Due to their strong defense of nesting territories, males can sometimes be lured into view with even pathetic imitations of their whistled songs. Annoyed by what they perceive to be an intruder, they switch to a sassy, low *tsk-dee-dee*.

Tufted Titmice nest in woodpecker holes, birdhouses and other cavities, forming a cup of grass, shredded bark, and leaves. Titmice are sometimes so desperate to collect hair to line their nests that they pull it from neighborhood dogs, passing deer, and even human heads. Eggs are laid in April. Clutches may contain as many as nine eggs, which are white and sparingly spotted. Incubation requires 12 to 14 days. The young fledge at 17 or 18 days of age, usually in May.

IDENTIFICATION TIPS
- ▶ climbs down trees head-first
- ▶ black cap is grayer in females
- ▶ white face with small black eyes

WHITE-BREASTED NUTHATCH
Sitta carolinensis

The *yank-yank-yank* voice of the White-breasted Nuthatch is common in oak-hickory woods in winter as well as summer. These five-inch, black, gray and white birds are the only tree climbers able to move head-first down tree trunks. This enables them to find insects in the bark that might be missed by "tree-up" gleaners such as woodpeckers. In addition to insects, they eat seeds that they press into crevices in bark and hack open with their bills. Early observers noticed this behavior and used it in their name. They often visit bird feeders, especially relishing sunflower seeds.

An adult pair will spend its entire life within a 25 to 50 acre patch of woods. Nuthatches nest in tree holes originally excavated by woodpeckers. Egg-laying commences from late April through May. They have surprisingly large clutches of up to ten eggs. Due to the protection afforded by the cavity, like other cavity nesters, White-breasted Nuthatches will rear nearly all of their young if food is available. Families are raised by July. There is no subsequent nesting during the year.

The sexes of White-breasted Nuthatches are nearly alike except for the male's blacker crown. To add a bit of confusion, there is a second nuthatch that occasionally migrates to the Midwest, the Red-breasted Nuthatch (*Sitta canadensis*). Red-breasted Nuthatches are slightly smaller and, as suggested by their name, their breasts are tinged with red. They are best distinguished from White-breasted Nuthatches, however, by a black stripe through the eye. More at home in the coniferous forests of the north and mountainous west, Red-breasted Nuthatches display an affinity for pines while here. They also visit bird feeders.

IDENTIFICATION TIPS
▶ large wren, about the size of a small sparrow
▶ warm rufous-brown above, bright buff-colored below
▶ conspicuous eyebrow stripe

CAROLINA WREN

Thryothorus ludovicianus

arolina Wrens exhibit the usual wren characteristics of a roundish body, fine bill and cocked tail. These wrens, however, are rusty with vivid, white eye-lines. And, although small, they are the largest wrens in the eastern United States. At five inches in length and seven ounces, they are double the weight of House Wrens. Carolina Wrens are well-known in the southeastern United States, south of a line extending from central Missouri to central Ohio. Their numbers diminish to the north of that line and they are essentially absent north of a line extending from southern Iowa through southern Michigan. They are non-migrating, permanent residents throughout their range.

Although distributed through only a portion of the Midwestern States Region, Carolina Wrens are included in this book because, where they do reside, they are often encountered. For rural residents within their range, Carolina Wrens are especially familiar because they frequent gardens and shrubs, and tend to build nests in farm implements, stored boats, firewood stacks, mail boxes, and hanging flower pots. People who are attentive to their ringing *tea kettle - tea kettle - tea kettle* call, hear them at all seasons and sometimes in the woods well away from human habitation.

Having occupied nesting territories through the winter, Carolina Wren pairs begin nest construction in March. Composed of grass, leaves, and feathers, these bulky structures are situated where protected from the weather. A typical clutch contains four to six eggs. The eggs are white with encircling speckles of brown. Incubation requires 15 days, and the young depart the nest at 12 to 14 days of age. Carolina Wrens nest as many as three times until as late September.

Because they are largely insectivorous and year-round residents, Carolina Wrens numbers are sometimes reduced by severe winter weather. On cold winter nights, people sometimes find them fluffed into unrecognizable puff balls under awnings and in sheds.

IDENTIFICATION TIPS
- ▶ small, energetic
- ▶ the plainest wren; unstreaked back; gray-brown
- ▶ distinguished from others by a light eye-ring and lack of facial striping

HOUSE WREN

Troglodytes aedon

Because of their affinity for yards and gardens, House Wrens are one of our best known birds. At a mere four-and-a-half inches in length, they are tiny packets of energy. Quivering, they burst forth with their bubbling, chattering songs usually from a perch within a few feet of the ground. Despite their usual boisterousness, they can become quiet when skulking through bushes and undergrowth hunting the small insects that constitute the majority of their diet. Only when there is a perceived danger, such as a human or pet, do they interrupt their foraging and rise in retaliation with a low, even rattle.

These small but mighty birds are cavity nesters and compete viciously for favorite sites, even to the point of sometimes pecking competing bird species to death. More commonly, however, upon arriving on the breeding ground in May, males claim nesting territories by filling the available cavities, such as birdhouses and woodpecker holes, with thorny twigs. When the female arrives a few days later, she chooses her favorite from among all the cavities that her mate has claimed. She busily removes the twigs and builds a cup lined with grasses, fibers and feathers. Here she deposits five to eight glossy-brown, speckled eggs. They hatch in 13 days and the young flutter from the hole around 17 days later. House wrens nest twice in a season. After the young are reared for the year, House Wrens fall silent before departing in September for their winter home in the southern United States and Mexico.

Many people enjoy providing birdhouses for House Wrens. An entrance hole the size of a quarter is just right to accommodate these small birds yet exclude competitors.

RUBY-CROWNED KINGLET

- ▶ distinguished from Golden-crowned by conspicuous eye ring
- ▶ small, slender bill
- ▶ stub-tailed
- ▶ ruby crown of male may be concealed
- ▶ hovers briefly; prefers conifers
- ▶ any kinglet without a crown patch and eye-stripe is this species

GOLDEN-CROWNED KINGLET

- ▶ brightly striped head separates it from other tiny woodland birds
- ▶ female has yellow crown, male has orange, both bordered by black
- ▶ small, slender bill
- ▶ both kinglets flick their strongly-barred wings upward

RUBY-CROWNED KINGLET
Regulus calendula

GOLDEN-CROWNED KINGLET
Regulus satrapa

ext to hummingbirds, kinglets are our smallest birds. Only four inches in length and weighing one-fourth ounce, Ruby-crowned Kinglets are known only as spring and fall migrants throughout all but the extreme northern Midwest. People that remain still, such as deer hunters in tree stands, often have a close look because kinglets seem fearless, sometimes approaching within a few feet. Olive-green, with an eye-ring, wingbars, and a light edging to the wing feathers, Ruby-crowned Kinglets characteristically flick their wings as they hop among the branches. They frequent trees offering dense cover such as cedars and pines. When capturing insects from the underside of leaves, they hover like hummingbirds. Only males possess the ruby crown that gives the species its name. The Ruby-crowned Kinglet's *tee-da-leet, tee-da-leet, tee-da-leet* song carries well considering their small size.

Golden-crowned Kinglets are slightly smaller than Ruby-crowned Kinglets. Like their "cousins," they are olive and have wingbars. However, they differ in having a white and black stripe above the eye. These stripes border a vivid yellow crown that in males has red in the middle. Their song is a complex series of rising notes followed by a descending *whip-lipalip*. Golden-crowned Kinglets are insectivorous like Ruby-crowned Kinglets but less likely to hover. Golden-crowned Kinglets also nest in the extreme northern parts of Minnesota, Wisconsin, and Michigan. Displaying their affinity for pines and spruce, they have been expanding their breeding range southward from northern coniferous forests into spruce plantations in Illinois, Indiana, and Ohio. Although best seen during migration, some spend the winter as far north as Lake Superior. Despite their size, they are able to survive nighttime temperatures of minus 50-degrees Fahrenheit.

Ruby-crowned

Golden-crowned

IDENTIFICATION TIPS
► tiny, slender, smaller than a chickadee
► blue-gray back, whitish below, white eye-ring
► extremely active
► long black-and-white tail is always twitching up
  and down or side to side

BLUE-GRAY GNATCATCHER

Polioptila caerulea

hese lively, four-inch birds are nearly as tiny as their cousins, the kinglets. The "blue-gray" part of their name accurately describes their color, but their identity is cinched when one sees the white outer feathers of their comparatively long, black tails. They also have a light eye ring. The "gnatcatcher" part of their name is fitting because they prey on small insects such as gnats, as well as inchworms and spiders. Foraging birds can be picked out high in trees as they flutter and dangle among the outer foliage. Their high, thin *zeees* and nasal *mews* are constant as they work. These sounds are easily learned although too high-pitched to be heard by some people.

Blue-gray Gnatcatchers winter along the Gulf Coast southward to Central America. They breed across the southern United States and their abundance trails off to the north of Missouri, Illinois, and Ohio. Because of their reliance on leaf-eating insects, they don't arrive on their breeding grounds until leaves have begun to emerge in spring.

Most Blue-gray Gnatcatchers nest along deciduous woodland edges, especially near streams. Nesting commences soon after their return in April. Nests are saddled high on horizontal limbs. They are composed of spider webs, plant fibers, and down, resulting in an elasticity that enables the nest to expand as the young grow. It is camouflaged on the outside with bits of lichen. Despite their concealing features, nests can usually be located by following the activities of parents. Into these two-inch-diameter cups, the female lays four to five minuscule, speckled eggs. The young hatch in 13 days and leave the nest 12 to 15 days later. The earliest nesting pairs may nest a second time during the season.

IDENTIFICATION TIPS

▶ a bit larger than a sparrow

▶ male has bright, entirely blue back and rusty throat and breast (the Indigo Bunting is all blue below)

▶ appears round-shouldered when perched

▶ female is duller than male

▶ juvenile is speckle-breasted, grayish, but with some blue in wings and tail

EASTERN BLUEBIRD
Sialia sialis

Bluebirds are perhaps the most loved birds in North America. Their appeal stems from their delightful songs and perceived gentleness and tameness, but mostly for the vivid blue plumage of males. Male Eastern Bluebirds are brilliant blue on the head, back, wings, and tail, contrasting with a deep-orange breast. Females have grayish-blue on the body in place of the male's rich blue. Both sexes are about six-and-a-half inches in length.

The landscapes in which Eastern Bluebirds reside are nearly as charming as the birds themselves. They favor areas dominated by expanses of short grass with a few trees. Pastures, cemeteries, parks, and golf courses offer suitable habitat. They avoid wooded suburbs and forests. They were perhaps at their zenith in the eastern states when the region was dominated by small, diversified farms; they have retreated to an extent as vast areas have become reforested. Still, where habitat is appropriate, Eastern Bluebirds remain common and their *cheer-cheery-up* songs can be heard from March through August.

Eastern Bluebirds return to their breeding territories in March. Males defend their claims with song and, when required, skirmishes with competing bluebirds. If the conflict is with a neighboring pair, the female will assist her mate by entering the fray against the female of the opposing pair. Bluebirds are dependent on woodpecker holes and other existing cavities for nesting. Many people have discovered the pleasure of providing them man-made nest boxes. The popularity of this hobby is perhaps the reason that bluebird numbers have been increasing in recent decades. If constructed with a one-and-a-half inch diameter entrance, European Starlings, notorious competitors for nest sites, are unable to enter. Eastern Bluebirds lay four to six light blue eggs that hatch in two weeks. The young fly from the nest at 15 to 18 days of age. Bluebirds regularly nest twice a season, the young fledging in May and again in June. In the southern part of their range, where the breeding season is longer, they occasionally nest a third time in late summer.

The Eastern Bluebird's list of assets includes the fact that they are economically beneficial. Over half of their summertime diet consists of grasshoppers and crickets. Though migratory, a few winter as far north as Iowa and Michigan. The Eastern Bluebird's popularity resulted in their selection as the State Bird of New York and Missouri.

IDENTIFICATION TIPS

▶ rusty head

▶ smaller than a Robin; plump

▶ distinguished from Brown Thrasher by round spots, dark eyes, and short tail; from other thrushes by the large round breast spots and deepening redness about the head

WOOD THRUSH

Hylocichla mustelina

ere it not for their songs, Wood Thrushes would be inconspicuous residents of our forests and wooded lots. Luckily for us, however, they do sing and their glorious arias emanate from the interior of rich forests throughout the eastern half of the United States. Even well-forested suburban areas may accommodate a Wood Thrush or two. They are most vocal from late April through July, especially at dawn and dusk. Their vocalizations are arguably the most beautiful of any North America bird. The natural harmony is derived from the concurrent use of two vocal organs, resulting in flute-like notes that have a clear, almost ethereal quality. Songs are delivered in two-second phrases that end in delightful trills. These are repeated ten or more times a minute.

These birds of the woodland understory are rusty-brown above with conspicuously-spotted white breasts and white eye-rings. They are eight inches long. They feed on insects and other invertebrates on the forest floor. Having wintered from Mexico to South America, Wood Thrushes are back on their breeding territories between late April and early May. Nests are composed of grass, leaves, and mud, and are usually situated in the fork of a lateral branch within five feet of the ground. Eggs are glossy blue-green. A standard clutch contains three to four eggs. Incubation requires 13 days and the young fledge two weeks later. They nest twice each season.

Where forests are small and scattered, the nests of forest birds like Wood Thrushes are more easily found by Brown-headed Cowbirds. Wood Thrushes behave naively, usually accepting the cowbird eggs as their own and hatching and rearing the foster young at the expense of their own. This is perhaps the reason that Wood Thrush numbers are declining throughout much of their range.

IDENTIFICATION TIPS
- ▶ dark gray back; brick-red breast
- ▶ head of female is paler than male's
- ▶ breast of juvenile is speckled, with a rust-colored wash

AMERICAN ROBIN

Turdus migratorius

obin "red-breasts" may very well be the best known birds in North America. Prevalent in yards and parks, they move quickly with a running skip, then stop abruptly to cock their heads. It has been suggested that they are listening for prey but they are more likely using one eye to watch for movement in the grass or at the surface of the soil. Robins especially relish earthworms, which they locate best in mown lawns and closely grazed pastures. They also eat various insects.

Today, American Robins range throughout almost all of North America. Two hundred years ago, however, before the advent of manicured lawns, they tended to be birds of the forest. But lawns and closely-grazed pastures provide such desirable habitat that their numbers increased and their range expanded. The introduction and spread of foreign earthworms may have also facilitated their range expansion because, in addition to using the worms themselves as food, they use the muddy worm castings to build nests.

Males, which have brighter breasts and darker upper-parts, claim territories from March through July with clear, liquid whistles and trills. If singing alone does not deter an interloper, a cock fight may ensue, culminating in the combatants thrashing about on the ground. Females alone construct the nests. Nests are built of mud and fine grasses, and are six inches across. They are usually situated in the fork of a tree, though occasionally on building ledges. There are typically four "robin's egg blue" eggs per clutch. It takes two weeks for the eggs to hatch and two more for the speckle-breasted young to leave the nest. Both parents feed the young. The first brood usually fledges in May or June and a second in June or July.

In winter, American Robins gather in flocks of up to a few hundred individuals that frequent woods, searching among the leaf litter for whatever insect remains they can find. They also eat the fruits of trees and shrubs. Highly nomadic, they avoid areas with prolonged snow cover; although, when conditions allow, they may winter as far north as Iowa, northern Illinois, and Michigan. Those people who see robins all winter are amused at those who cite the first robin as a harbinger of spring.

The American Robin is the State Bird of Michigan and Wisconsin.

IDENTIFICATION TIPS

▶ slim; slate-gray with distinct black cap

▶ the chestnut undertail may not be noticeable

▶ flips tail jauntily

▶ no other bird is plain dark gray with rusty
underparts

GRAY CATBIRD

Dumetella carolinensis

Gray Catbirds were named for their mewing sounds, which are only a part of their highly diverse repertoire. They also emit squeaks, whines, and rasps, often as a rambling discourse during which the same sound is seldom heard twice in succession. Using both sides of its vocal apparatus independently, a single bird is capable of singing two very different songs at the same time. As if to further confuse an observer, Gray Catbirds incorporate the sounds of other birds from the neighborhood, and typically sing from the interior of a tree or bush so that an observer sees only a bit of the songster when it moves. Despite all of these challenges to identification, they are one of the easiest birds to identify because, taken together, these singing characteristics make them unique.

Gray Catbirds are charcoal gray all over with a black cap and a patch of rust below at the base of the tail. Their wings are rather short and a long tail attributes to their eight-inch length. The sexes are indistinguishable. Gray Catbirds eat a variety of insects and numerous small berries. Rarely, they can be attracted to feeding stations with cut-up oranges and other fruits.

Gray Catbirds winter along the Gulf Coast, in the Caribbean, and in Central America, and return to their nesting grounds from mid-April through May. They nest from the East Coast westward through the Rockies, favoring bushes. They are commonly found in ornamental shrubs and hedges in yards. Nesting ensues soon after they return. Their bulky nests are typically well-hidden in thickets, briars, or dense trees. Commonly, four eggs are laid. They are glossy, greenish-blue and hatch after 13 days of incubation. The young leave the nest 11 to 13 days later, usually in early June. A second nesting follows with the young fledging in July.

IDENTIFICATION TIPS

▶ white wing patches show clearly during flight; wingbeats are slow enough to be counted

▶ slimmer and longer-tailed than Robin; slender bill

▶ flicks tail from side to side

NORTHERN MOCKINGBIRD

Mimus polyglottos

These familiar residents of yards and parks are renowned for their ability to mimic the songs of other birds. Tireless songsters, they sing nearly the year around and, during the full moon, even around the clock. They characteristically perch in the uppermost tip of a tree or bush and deliver a rapid-fire series of identical sounds before switching to an entirely different series. Snippets from birds such as robins, phoebes, cardinals, and quail might be incorporated into their songs along with whistles, *chats*, and *mews*, and the occasional barking dog or squeaking gate. Listeners might be fooled briefly before realizing that the renditions are too rapid and repetitive to be real.

Despite their bewildering diversity, Northern Mockingbird songs apparently serve the same function as those of most songbirds: to attract mates and to defend territories from members of their own species. Prized territories contain berry bushes and are most strongly defended as the fruit sweetens, even in fall and winter. Known for their pugnacity, Northern Mockingbirds aggressively harass any animal that they consider a threat, including crows, cats, and sometimes people.

Although the look-alike female also sings, the male is most vocal. When courting, he sings in flight. Males that encounter each other at territory boundaries perform a "boundary dance" in which they leap upward while flashing their white wing patches. Pairing occurs in fall, and nesting is underway as early as March. Nests are bulky, composed of thorny sticks, and hidden in trees, shrubs, or vines. Mockingbird eggs are brownish and blotched, and average four per clutch. The female alone incubates the eggs for the required 12 to 13 days. The stubby-tailed young leave the nest at 12 days of age. Mockingbirds nest a second time during the summer, and newly-fledged young may show up as late as August.

Northern Mockingbirds are most numerous in the southern states although, in recent decades, they have expanded northward to Iowa, Wisconsin, and Michigan. Their familiarity in the south has resulted in their selection as the State Bird of Arkansas, Mississippi, Tennessee, and Texas.

IDENTIFICATION TIPS

▶ rich, rufous brown above, heavily streaked below

▶ wing bars, curved bill, long tail, yellow eye

▶ most often confused with Wood Thrush (which has shorter tail and dark eyes)

▶ song is similar to Catbird's, but each phrase is given twice rather than once or many times (mockingbird)

BROWN THRASHER

Toxostoma rufum

These long-tailed, rusty birds are usually seen flying short distances within a few feet of brushy cover along rural roads and in overgrown, brushy fields. Sometimes they visit suburban yards where hedges and ornamental bushes simulate shrubby rural habitat. Although Brown Thrashers resemble Wood Thrushes in appearance, they are separated by habitat, the latter being a bird of the forest. Additionally, Brown Thrashers are longer, half of their ten inches being tail, and have streaks versus spots on their breasts.

Like other mimic thrushes, such as Gray Catbirds and Northern Mockingbirds, Brown Thrashers are vocal with loud, diverse *squawks, peeps, mews,* and whistles. Though usually heard before seen because of the brushy cover in which they reside, Brown Thrashers are relatively easy to identify because of their unique songs. They tend to give the same phrase twice in succession. In contrast, Gray Catbirds sing one phrase then switch to another, and Northern Mockingbirds repeat a series.

Brown Thrashers eat beetles, other insects, and fruits such as blackberries, elderberries, and grapes. In winter, most retreat to the southeastern states. During March and April, Brown Thrashers return to their breeding grounds, which extend throughout the entire eastern two-thirds of the United States.

Singing and pairing commences immediately upon their return. Nests are usually well-hidden near the ground in bushes or vines. They are bulky structures composed of twigs. Brown Thrashers nest twice each breeding season, in April through May, and June through July. First clutches typically consist of four eggs, second clutches, three. Nest construction requires about four days, incubation 13, and the nestling stage, another 12. The female alone incubates the glossy, red-speckled eggs. Both parents, which look alike, feed the young.

Following nesting, in August, Brown Thrashers become quiet as the new young strike out on their own and the adults molt into a fresh plumage. Brown Thrashers quietly depart for the south in September and October.

IDENTIFICATION TIPS

▶ distinguished from blackbirds by its short tail and its browner wings (show best in flight)

▶ yellow bill is diagnostic in spring and summer; winter plumage is heavily speckled and bill is darker

▶ flies swiftly and directly, not rising and falling like most blackbirds

EUROPEAN STARLING

Sturnus vulgaris

uropean Starlings are stout, six-inch birds that walk rather than hop. In flight, their wings appear translucent and a star-like silhouette results from the pointed combination of wings, head, and tail. For a few months following their annual fall molt, the black adults are speckled with tan and white. The speckles are actually light-colored feather tips. Through the year, they gradually wear off until by spring the birds are left with a black plumage that gleams green and lavender in various lights. Bills are yellow except in juveniles, which have dark bills and a uniformly brown plumage.

During their spring and summer breeding season, these gregarious birds emit assorted squeaks, trills, and rattles. They stuff their bulky nests into available holes, often in buildings. When using tree cavities, they may displace native hole-nesters, such as bluebirds. Their eggs are light blue and number four to six per clutch. Although their sharp bills are regularly used to take insects from lawns, these adaptable birds sometimes behave as swallows, catching insects high overhead. This is especially common in fall after the swallows have departed. In winter, they gather into immense, noisy flocks lining power lines.

European Starlings are so plentiful and widespread that it is difficult to believe that they are not native to North America. Their origin can be traced to 100 birds that were released in New York City's Central Park in 1890 and 1891. The organization involved was dedicated to the establishment of foreign birds in New York State and had successfully introduced House Sparrows 40 years earlier. A few years following their release, European Starlings began to expand their range westward. They reached Ohio by 1916, Missouri by 1929, and the Rocky Mountains by 1940. They now range from coast to coast, occupying such diverse habitats as city centers, farms, fields, and forests.

Their great versatility in nesting behavior and food habits contributed to their successful colonization of North America. In addition to fruits and seeds, European Starlings eat garbage, livestock feeds, and some crops. They also occasionally monopolize bird feeders, a problem that can usually be controlled by providing only sunflower seeds.

IDENTIFICATION TIPS

▶ sleek, crested, brown bird with a yellowish belly; larger than a House Sparrow
▶ yellow band at the tail tip
▶ juvenile is grayer, softly streaked below
▶ fly in compact flocks; seldom seen alone
   except when nesting
▶ often indulge in fly-catching
▶ sexes similar

CEDAR WAXWING
Bombycilla cedrorum

hrough much of the year, Cedar Waxwings occur in foraging flocks of one hundred or more individuals. Relishing berries, they search them out whenever they are the sweetest and most succulent. Huge hackberry trees can be stripped of fruit in a matter of minutes by a horde of these energetic birds. Though classified as songbirds, Cedar Waxwings are incapable of producing anything resembling a song. Instead they emit tiny, buzzing *zeees* as they feed and fly about. This sound is usually the first clue that they are around. Upon looking up, an observer may be able to pick out an individual's pointed crest and the yellow tip of its tail. Binoculars are needed to witness the full beauty of these immaculate, six-inch birds. Their appealing features include a softly-hued plumage, black mask, and the startlingly red "wax droplets" on the wings that give them their name.

Cedar Waxwings live year round throughout most of North America. Flocks separate into pairs in June, July, and August to commence nesting. The extreme lateness of nesting is timed to match the ripening of the local fruit. In addition to berries, they catch flying insects, especially when feeding young. Nests are grass-made cups situated on horizontal limbs. Four to five gray, spotted eggs require 12 days of incubation. Another two weeks pass before the young fledge.

Nesting is seldom witnessed as compared to the conspicuous, nomadic flocks that invade neighborhoods to harvest the fruits of trees and shrubs. Favorites include cedars, dogwoods, cherries, hawthorns, crab-apples, hollies, and mulberries. Sometimes in spring, individuals become intoxicated on old berries that have become fermented by warming temperatures. They periodically collide with window panes, perhaps as a result of this affliction.

IDENTIFICATION TIPS

▶ bright yellow rump, yellow patch on crown and on front of each wing

▶ spring male: blue-gray above, heavy black breast patch

▶ spring female: brownish, basic pattern similar

▶ winter: brownish above, whitish below, streaked, yellow rump

▶ also called "Myrtle" Warbler

YELLOW-RUMPED WARBLER

Dendroica coronata

Of the nearly 40 wood warbler species that nest in or visit the Midwest, Yellow-rumped Warblers are one of the most common and ubiquitous. Although only five inches in length, these active birds can often be glimpsed and identified among the foliage because of the vivid yellow spots on the male's shoulders, crown and rump. The presence of white tail-spots, white wing-bars and a black chest-band help to clarify the identification of these delightful blue-gray birds. Although much more subdued in color, females also possess the wing-bars and yellowish rump.

Yellow-rumped Warblers are relatively easy to detect because of their tendency to forage in well-forested neighborhoods and in trees along the woodland edge. Their primary migratory period, March and April, proceeds the emergence of greenery, a notorious hindrance to most warbler watching. Careful observation will reveal them gleaning and fly-catching insects among the branches. Where one is seen, there are usually a few others of both sexes.

By mid-May they have departed for their nesting range, which spans the northern coniferous forests from New England to the Great Lakes and across Canada to Alaska. Following nesting, they molt into the duller plumage that they wear when they return to us in late September. They linger until November. Some spend the winter in the southern Midwest, surviving on berries and the few insects they can find. Wintering birds also feed on the sap oozing from tree wounds.

IDENTIFICATION TIPS

▶ abundant in moist grassy or shrubby areas
▶ black mask distinguishes the male
▶ female and immature are olive-brown with bright yellow throat, buff-yellow breast; no black mask
▶ seen near or on the ground
▶ song repeated several times
▶ separated from similar warblers by whitish belly and brownish sides

♂

♀

COMMON YELLOWTHROAT

Geothlypis trichas

O f all the wood warblers in North America, Common Yellowthroats are the most numerous and widespread breeders. They are also the most peculiarly marked. Although females of this four-and-a-half-inch warbler are a simple drab-olive, males have black masks and vivid yellow throats that identify them with certainty. Seeing them can be difficult, however, because these are birds of the thicket. But the attentive birdwatcher can quite easily pick out their unique *which-ity which-ity which-ity* calls and then spot the little songster within the top of a clump of vegetation.

These warblers favor the brushy countryside, especially where there is profuse, low vegetation in damp areas. Prime habitats are the brushy draws of pastures and the willows and reeds that border streams, lakes, and ponds. Careful observation may discern the little "bandits" flitting among the vegetation within a few feet of the ground. It is usually not until the male decides to sing from the tip of a bush that there is an opportunity to see him well. But the opportunity is fleeting as these active birds apparently have a full agenda. Common Yellowthroats eat small insects and spiders that they glean from vegetation.

Common Yellowthroats return to their breeding range in late April, having wintered along the Gulf Coast and southward through the Caribbean and Central America. They are one of a very few warblers whose breeding range extends across North America. Nests are concealed near the ground and often composed of the same vegetation that supports them so that they blend with the surroundings. Three to five eggs constitute a clutch. They are a mere three-fourths of an inch in length, and white with speckles encircling the larger end. They hatch in 12 days; the young leave the nest in another 12. Both parents feed the growing young until they are totally independent at around 30 days of age. There is only one nesting per season.

SUMMER TANAGER
- ► male is rose-red all over with a yellowish bill; no crest
- ► female is olive above and deep yellow below
- ► young males acquiring adult plumage may be patched with red and green
- ► female is orange-yellow, while Scarlet Tanager is more yellow-green with darker wings
- ► female orioles have wing bars

Summer Tanager ♂

Scarlet Tanager ♂

SCARLET TANAGER
- ► male is flaming scarlet with jet black wings and tail (no other North American bird has a red body with black wings and tail); in July-August, red feathers are replaced with greenish ones; black wings remain
- ► first year males occasionally more orange than red
- ► female, immature, and winter male are a dull greenish above, yellowish below, with dark brown/black wings

SUMMER TANAGER
Piranga rubra

SCARLET TANAGER
Piranga olivacea

 ummer Tanagers are those solid red birds seen in the woods that are not Northern Cardinals. In contrast to cardinals, they lack the crest and their bill is not nearly as massive. These six-inch birds are more common in the southern parts of the Midwest. Despite their brilliance, often the only evidence of their presence is their lengthy, rising and falling roundelays coming from the forest canopy. The song is similar to the American Robin's but somewhat sweeter. In addition, Summer Tanagers produce *chick-tuck* or *chicky-tuck-tuck* sounds.

One of the most brilliant birds anywhere is the adult male Scarlet Tanager. His vivid red plumage, contrasting with black wings and tail, is a treat for the eyes, especially against a background of green leaves. They are more commonly seen in the northern Midwest. In the south they tend to live in the forest interior. Despite their brilliance, their association with large trees makes them even more difficult to see than Summer Tanagers. Like their cousins, Scarlet Tanagers also deliver robin-like songs but, compared to the Summer's song, theirs are hoarse as though the bird has a bur in its throat.

Females and juveniles of both species are yellowish in place of red. Maturing males are blotched with red as they molt into adult plumage. Both Summer and Scarlet Tanagers winter with a multitude of tropical tanagers in Central and South America. They return to North America to breed around the end of April and depart in September. Their nests are constructed by the females high in trees and rarely seen. A month-and-a-half is required to raise a family. They nest only once a season. Tanager nests are occasionally parasitized by Brown-headed Cowbirds.

Tanagers sometimes visit hummingbird feeders. They can be attracted to cut-up citrus fruits placed out on deck railings.

Summer Tanager  Scarlet Tanager

IDENTIFICATION TIPS

▶ smaller and more slender than a Robin

▶ head and upper parts black, rusty sides, white belly, long rounded tail with large white spots; female is similar but black areas are replaced with brown

▶ adult's iris is red; immature's is brown

▶ rummages noisily among dead leaves

EASTERN TOWHEE

Pipilo erythrophthalmus

Despite the snazzy plumage of the male, Eastern Towhees are more often heard than seen. Their rhythmic *drink-your-tee-ee-ee-ee-ee* songs emanate from rural woodland edges and brushy fields from April through July. Towhees are best observed by searching for these songsters amongst the foliage of trees or bushes. Brassy *chewink* calls reveal the locations of individuals hidden among brush and briars.

Upon sighting one of these seven-and-a-half-inch songbirds for the first time, the observer may notice the rusty color beneath and be reminded of an American Robin. But more careful observation will reveal that this color is only on the sides. Their former name, "Rufous-sided Towhee," is a fitting description of their appearance. The head, back, wings, and tail are black on males and brown on females. The tails of Eastern Towhees are relatively long and rounded, with white outer corners. Their flight is typically low and of short distance as they flutter from one hiding place to another.

Eastern Towhees occupy the eastern half of the United States beginning with their arrival in March until their departure in late fall. They feed on beetles, millipedes, sow bugs, spiders, snails, and seeds. Food is uncovered by the peculiar method of scratching through leaves with both feet at once. People who are able to attract them to bird feeders may observe the same two-footed scratching technique beneath the feeder.

Eastern Towhees build bulky nests, well-hidden in bushes, either on or within a few feet of the ground. Their three to five cream-colored, speckled eggs hatch in 12 days and the young leave the nest by day ten, well before they can fly.

IDENTIFICATION TIPS

▶ in general, head and breast patterns are most helpful for identifying sparrows; also the length and shape of the tail

FIELD SPARROW

▶ rusty cap; pink bill and legs
▶ clear breast
▶ less noticeable facial striping than other rusty-capped sparrows
▶ narrow, light eye-ring
▶ no dark eye line

Field Sparrow

Chipping Sparrow

CHIPPING SPARROW

▶ bright rusty cap
▶ gray-breasted
▶ black line through the eye with a white line over it
▶ black bill and very white eye stripe distinguish it
▶ common on lawns

FIELD SPARROW
Spizella pusilla

CHIPPING SPARROW
Spizella passerina

ield Sparrows are rural birds, common in brushy pastures and scrublands throughout the eastern half of the United States. As is usual for sparrows, they are most often detected and identified by sound rather than sight. The Field Sparrow's song is a whistled trill that starts slowly and increases in rapidity with the rhythm of a dropped coin jingling to a stop. Visually, these five-inch birds are distinguished from most other sparrows by their pinkish bills, white eye-rings, unstreaked breasts, and rusty caps. Field Sparrows return from the southern states in March. Nests are five-inch diameter grass cups constructed near the ground in shrubs. Eggs are pale blue with a ring of reddish speckles on the larger end. They number three to four and hatch in 11 days. The young leave the nest 13 days later. Field Sparrows nest two or three times a season.

Chipping Sparrows are commonly seen hopping about lawns in residential areas and parks. At four-and-a-half inches in length, they are so tiny as to be half hidden in the grass. Identifying features include a dark bill, rusty cap, white eye-line, two white wing-bars and a plain breast. Their song is usually the first evidence of their presence, but most people would probably dismiss it as the sound of an insect. It is a high-pitched, rapid series of even chips, usually delivered from a low perch such as a fence or bush. Having wintered in the Gulf Coast states, they spread across the continent during April and nesting quickly ensues. Their four-inch diameter grass nests are typically situated in ornamental shrubs, hedges, or small trees, especially evergreens. Hair from pets, livestock, and even people is used as lining. Their tiny eggs are glossy-blue with black speckles on the larger end. A typical clutch of four eggs requires ten days of incubation, and the young fledge ten days later. As with Field Sparrows, Chipping Sparrows are regularly victimized by Brown-headed Cowbirds.

Field Sparrow   Chipping Sparrow

IDENTIFICATION TIPS

▶ heavily streaked breast with a large, central spot

▶ no yellow or buffy colors

▶ pumps its long, slightly rounded tail as it flies

SONG SPARROW

Melospiza melodia

The most memorable aspect of Song Sparrows, as should be expected from their common and scientific names, is their song. They are more likely heard than seen and people who take the time to discern one bird sound from another are most likely to notice Song Sparrows. These six-inch birds are common and their trilling *maids-maids-maids - put on your teakettle-ettle-ettle* might be heard coming from brushy draws and stream side thickets from March through August. By keying in on the sound, the actual songster may be found, usually toward the top of a bush. They are recognized by their heavily streaked breasts with a spot in the middle.

Song Sparrows winter throughout all but the northern edge of the lower 48 states. They would be inconspicuous at that season if it were not for their tendency to form flocks. They eat waste grains and sometimes visit bird feeders. By March, Song Sparrows have left the southern states and occupy a breeding range that extends from coast to coast and to the northern extent of trees in Canada. They feed primarily on insects during the growing season.

Nests are typically well-hidden on or near the ground in thick vegetation. Their three to six eggs are pale green and heavily speckled. The eggs hatch in two weeks and the young leave the nest ten days later, a few days before being able to fly. Song Sparrows nest two to three times a breeding season.

Though not shown, Fox Sparrows (*Passerella iliaca*) are similar to Song Sparrows in having streaked breasts with a spot at the center. They, however, are rustier in color and are large sparrows at six to seven inches in length. They nest far to the north and occur in the Midwest only in migration and in winter. They often feed on the ground beneath bird feeders.

WHITE-CROWNED SPARROW

- ▶ pink or yellowish bill
- ▶ clear gray throat and breast
- ▶ puffy crown is prominently streaked with black and white
- ▶ shuns the woodland thickets that the White-throated Sparrow favors
- ▶ White-throated Sparrow is browner, has a well-defined white throat, yellow spot before the eye, black bill

White-crowned Sparrow

White-throated Sparrow

WHITE-THROATED SPARROW

- ▶ well-defined white throat
- ▶ yellow spot before the eye, black bill, short-necked posture
- ▶ seldom found far from dense cover
- ▶ usually feeds on the ground

WHITE-CROWNED SPARROW
Zonotrichia leucophrys

WHITE-THROATED SPARROW
Zonotrichia albicollis

These closely-related sparrows are common spring and fall migrants throughout most of the country. They are large for sparrows, being nearly six inches in length. Their streaked heads and solid gray breasts distinguish them from other sparrows, at least when in adult, springtime breeding plumage. The differences between these two "cousins" are explained by their names — White-throated Sparrows have white throats and White-crowned Sparrows have boldly black and white streaked crowns with prominent white centers. Fall and immature individuals have subtly streaked breasts and are generally more subdued.

The best way to identify these sparrows is by their songs. The White-throated Sparrow's is especially easy to remember. It is a high, clear whistle with a slow cadence of *Oh Sweet Canada Canada Canada*. It is heard the year around but the fall and winter version is sporadic and weak. The White-crowned Sparrow's song also contains clear whistles but it is more complex and buzzy. Some of its song segments are inherited whereas others are picked up at a few months of age by listening to adults. Their noticeable regional dialects are probably the result of songs being learned from parents.

White-crowned Sparrows breed in the Canadian far north and through much of the western United States. White-throated Sparrows nest across much of Canada but also into the northern portions of Minnesota, Wisconsin, and Michigan, and throughout most of New York and New England. They nest on or near the ground at woodland edges and lay three to five brown eggs. Through most of the Midwest, however, both of these sparrow species are mainly seen from October through April, and invariably in flocks with other sparrows. They often associate with bird feeding stations where they favor the spillage on the ground. White-throated Sparrows in migration favor brushy woodlands, while White-crowned Sparrows frequent more open woods. Both sparrows move about slowly and are easy to see.

White-crowned   White-throated

- ▶ uniformly slate gray; sparrow-shaped
- ▶ belly is whitish; bill is whitish/pinkish
- ▶ white outer tail feathers flash conspicuously when it flies
- ▶ males may have blackish hoods; females and immatures are duller

DARK-EYED JUNCO

Junco hyemalis

These six-inch, immaculate, gray birds with the white bellies are most noticed in winter as they scatter from roadside brush, flashing their trademark white outer tail feathers. Males are darker gray than females, and first-winter young are streaked and washed with brown. Juncos visit bird feeders where they hop about, scratching and pecking at the spillage, favoring millet and cracked sunflower seeds. They also eat the seeds of weeds and grasses. These "snow birds" forage in loose flocks while emitting jingling twitters to keep in contact. Some individuals serve as sentinels while others concentrate on food-finding. These duties change off as they work their way through the underbrush.

Dark-eyed Juncos range throughout the United States in winter. For a few weeks in March and April, just before departing their wintering grounds, males select uncharacteristically high perches from which to deliver their trilling courtship songs. They favor cool, wooded areas for nesting. They summer throughout the forested region of Canada and south through the northern portions of Minnesota, Wisconsin, and Michigan. Juncos construct nests on the ground at the base of a tree, beside a log, or by hiding it in some other way. Their four to five eggs are glossy light-blue with a dense speckling of brown on the large end. They hatch in 12 days. Dark-eyed Juncos nest twice each breeding season.

Bird banding has indicated that, though breeding and wintering ranges are often separated by hundreds of miles, individuals are capable of finding their way back year after year to winter in precisely the same yard.

IDENTIFICATION TIPS

▶ bright red, crested male with black face mask
   is unmistakable
▶ thick, red, conical beak is distinctive
▶ female is also crested, but yellowish-buff-
   brown with red on wings and tail
▶ immature is similar to female, but with a
   blackish bill

NORTHERN CARDINAL
Cardinalis cardinalis

Male Northern Cardinals are one of the most splendid birds in North America. Sometimes it takes a visitor from abroad or from the western United States, where there are no cardinals, to remind us to appreciate them despite their commonness. Even the females, with their warm hues and reddish wings, tails, and topknots, are beautiful in their own subtle way. One of the noticeable features of these eight-inch birds is their heavy bill. These instruments enable them to crack almost any seed coat. They especially favor sunflower seeds. Cardinals visit sunflower bird feeders, particularly during snowy weather and even in the dim light of early morning and late evening.

The Northern Cardinal's song is as appealing as its appearance. It is a series of clear, loud whistles, often given from a neighborhood treetop. The repertoire is diverse, resulting in regional dialects and even songs that are suited for different habitats. Cardinals in deep forests sing slower and lower notes, apparently to enhance transmission. Careful listeners will notice that males near to each other will copy each other's songs, sometimes going so far as to sing duets. This apparently indicates a mutual respect for territory boundaries. Males and females sometimes sing together during courtship and nesting.

Northern Cardinals range northward to southern Minnesota, Wisconsin, and Michigan, and from the East Coast to the High Plains of western Kansas and Nebraska. A peninsula of their population extends through much of the Desert Southwest. They are with us throughout the year and an individual may spend its entire life within a few acres. Nest building, typically low in a shrub, takes place in April and May. The two to five speckled eggs hatch in 12 days. The young leave the nest in ten days, when still too gray and stubby to be recognized as cardinals unless a parent is seen feeding them. They are able to fly well within a few days. Cardinals nest up to three times a season.

The extreme popularity of the Northern Cardinal is seen in its selection as State Bird by more states than any other bird: Illinois, Indiana, Ohio, Kentucky, North Carolina, Virginia and West Virginia.

IDENTIFICATION TIPS

▶ rose bib of adult male is diagnostic

▶ thick, pale bill

▶ in flight, white flashes across the black upper plumage and rose wing linings are visible

▶ female is streaked, like a large sparrow or female purple finch; recognized by the large, thick bill, broad white wing bars, striped crown, and broad white eyebrow stripe; females wing linings are orange-yellow and conspicuous in flight

♂

♀

ROSE-BREASTED GROSBEAK

Pheucticus ludovicianus

here are few events that provoke more excitement and curiosity among bird watchers than the first sighting of a Rose-breasted Grosbeak. Though fairly common, these attractive birds are only occasionally glimpsed. If a feeding station is operated in summer, that is the most likely place to see them. As with most birds, the males are the attention-getters. Their contrasting black and white coloration and rose bibs are splendid when seen against a background of green leaves. When in flight, a rose hue can be seen on the underside of the wings. The brown-streaked females are so different from the males that they might be mistaken for another species, unless it is noticed that they too are about eight inches long and have the same heavy, conical bills. These immense bills are used to crack tough shells and pods. They also eat buds, catkins, fruit, caterpillars, and moths. Their song is robin-like.

Rose-breasted Grosbeaks live in the eastern half of North America. After having wintered in South America, they migrate northward through the southeastern states in late April and May to their nesting ground, which extends from central Missouri and the Ohio River Valley northward into southern Canada. Any wooded area is acceptable for nesting, whether a suburban yard or small woodlot. In the southern reaches of their breeding range, they favor woods along rivers or in other damp areas.

Nests are constructed of grass stems or twigs and are hidden among leaves in the fork of a tree or bush. A clutch contains three to six eggs, which are glossy blue and heavily blotched with purple and brown, mostly on the large end. The parents alternate in incubating the eggs. Both feed the young for the ten days that they are growing in the nest and for several days after they first fly. Although they usually nest only once a season, in the southern part of their range, where the nesting season is longer, they sometimes fit in a second brood. Rose-breasted Grosbeaks are frequent hosts to Brown-headed Cowbirds.

IDENTIFICATION TIPS

▶ common in hedgerows and wood margins; perch on wires during nesting season

▶ male is brilliant, iridescent blue all over, darker on the crown, no wing bars

▶ female is plain brown with a tinge of blue on the tail and shoulder; she is devoid of obvious stripes, wing bars, or other marks

▶ female's unstreaked back separates them from all sparrows

▶ in fall, the male becomes more like the female, but some blue remains in the wings and tail

INDIGO BUNTING

Passerina cyanea

These are the small, solid-blue, finch-sized birds that can be seen along woodland edges throughout the rural areas of the Midwest. The solid-blue birds are the males, as females are a dusky brown. Males are so blue as to appear almost iridescent. Despite their abundance and brilliance, Indigo Buntings are not well known. Although they are among our most vocal birds, most people never notice them.

Beginning with their arrival in May, Indigo Buntings are heard almost constantly when in their habitat, even through the hot afternoons of July and August. The male's song is a strident ramble that rises and falls over a period of two to three seconds. Listening carefully, one can hear that most notes are paired. Though largely insectivorous, they also eat small seeds, berries, and buds. Males sometimes become so conflicted by the need to both eat and vocally defend their territories that they sing with food in their bills.

These four-and-a-half-inch songbirds are secretive when they choose, hiding among undergrowth and weedy tangles. Females especially adopt this habit when near their nests. Indigo Buntings nest twice during their summer stay. Females build a small, grass cup low in dense cover. They lay two to six glossy white eggs. Each nesting takes a little over a month. Brown-headed Cowbirds often lay their eggs in the nests of Indigo Buntings.

Like most songbirds, Indigo Buntings migrate at night. In a classic study of migration, those ready to depart Mexico's Yucatan Peninsula in spring were placed in cages in a planetarium in which a night sky was projected. Remarkably, most tried to fly against the side of the cage that faced the artificially created northern constellations, indicating that Indigo Buntings instinctively use celestial cues to determine the proper migration direction.

IDENTIFICATION TIPS

▶ about the size of a House Sparrow

▶ male looks like a small Meadowlark, with a black bib on a yellow chest (in fall, the bib is obscure or lacking)

▶ female is very similar to a female House Sparrow, except paler with a much lighter stripe over the eye and a touch of yellow on the breast; also a chestnut shoulder patch

▶ winter Dickcissel can be distinguished from House Sparrow by the chestnut wing patch, narrow streak at the side of the throat, and a trace of yellow

DICKCISSEL
Spiza americana

ickcissels may take the prize for being the commonest yet least known bird species in the Midwest. When hearing their name for the first time, some people think it is too strange for the bird to be real. Yet these six-inch finches are one of the most easily observed rural birds, especially in western parts of the Midwest. They are most associated with grassy or weedy fields, especially where there are bushes in which to nest. Territorial males perch just above the thick vegetation on fences, flower stems, or shrubs, where their yellow chests with the black bibs catch an observer's eye. Due to this color combination, they resemble miniature meadowlarks, a species that, interestingly, often lives in the same fields. While perched in this manner, males repeatedly lay claim to their patch of land with a wiry, unmusical trill that has the cadence of *dick-dick-dick-sissel*. The calling commences upon the males' return in early May, and continues through the heat of summer.

Dickcissels eat weed seeds, waste grains, and insects. In contrast to their rather scattered distribution when on their North American breeding ground, they assemble into such dense flocks in winter that much of their entire population is concentrated in only a few agricultural areas. Flocks containing millions have been devastating to Venezuelan rice producers and, although now illegal, those farmers in the past have declared open warfare on Dickcissels with firearms and dynamite.

Upon returning to their breeding range, Dickcissels scatter to appropriate fields extending from central Kansas to Ohio and from the Texas coast to Canada. About ten days following the males' appearance, the females arrive. Much the drabber sex, females are brown-streaked with only a hint of ochre on the chest. They are seldom seen because, unlike the territorial males, they must busy themselves with nest building and caring for the eggs and young. They receive little assistance from their mates, who may have one or more additional females. Cup nests are concealed in shrubs or clumps of grass. The three to five eggs are pale blue and require 12 to 13 days to hatch. The young venture from the nest after little more than a week. Dickcissels raise two broods each summer.

IDENTIFICATION TIPS

▶ spring male is the only North America land
   bird that is solid black below and light above
▶ female and fall male resemble large sparrows,
   but have buff-colored crown stripes and
   breasts, and narrow pointed tail feathers
▶ female resembles the female Red-winged
   Blackbird, but doesn't have the Red-wings'
   heavy breast striping

BOBOLINK

Dolichonyx oryzivorus

 ompared to other birds, the coloration of Bobolinks is upside down, with the color on their backs and not on their breasts. Males of this seven-inch member of the blackbird family are black except for a patch of yellow on the back of the head and white markings on their shoulders and rump. Females, as well as males in fall, are entirely buff and, on the rare occasions that they come out of hiding and are seen, they are usually dismissed as some kind of sparrow. Bobolink males are most often detected by the bubbling songs they deliver while fluttering above the grassy fields selected for nesting.

There are few birds so limited to grasslands as Bobolinks. Not just any grass will do, however. It must be thick and at least two feet tall. Usually it must be several acres in size so that it will accommodate at least a small nesting colony. Damp meadows are especially favored, as are hayfields or oats with a component of clover or alfalfa.

Having wintered in the vast grasslands of Argentina, Bobolinks journey 5,000 miles northward in small flocks, arriving in the southeastern states in March and April. They quickly pass through this hot, humid region, spreading out to colonize suitable grasslands in the cooler, northern states from Maine to Oregon, usually during May. In the Midwest, it is rare to find nesting Bobolinks south of Interstate 70. Although largely insectivorous, Bobolinks consume a variety of seeds, including grains such as oats and rice.

Nests are constructed on or near the ground in dense vegetation. Clutches average five to six eggs. Eggs are bronze with brown blotches and they hatch in 13 days. Each male may mate with one to several females. Occasionally, he will assist his primary mate with rearing the young while his secondary mates receive no assistance. The final egg in a clutch is laid a day after incubation begins so that it hatches a day later. This day-younger nestling can be sacrificed in situations where food is limited, such as for those females that do not receive male help. This increases the chance that the remaining young are reared successfully. To add confusion, however, it is known that the young in a female's nest may be fathered by different males. Young achieve flight in July. Bobolinks nest only once each year.

IDENTIFICATION TIPS

▶ male is all black with red and yellow shoulder stripes that are most conspicuous in spring (red is usually hidden during rest of the year)

▶ female is brownish with well-defined dark stripings below; they are longer billed and more heavily streaked than sparrows

▶ feed, fly, and roost in huge flocks

RED-WINGED BLACKBIRD

Agelaius phoeniceus

ales of this widespread species are readily recognized by their red shoulder patches. Territorial individuals flare these "epaulets" almost as headlights when coming in for a landing. When perched, they display them while delivering squawky *onk-a-ree* songs simultaneous with the slight spreading of wings and tail. When not behaving territorially, the shoulder coloration may be overlain with black feathers to the extent that only its yellow border shows. As compared to the nine-inch males, females are so small and brown-streaked as to resemble sparrows. Both sexes produce a *check-check-check* call while flying in flocks overhead or when their nests are approached too closely.

Red-winged Blackbirds are believed to be the most common birds in North America. This is surprising to most city dwellers until they realize that these blackbirds occur nearly throughout the continent and in rural habitats ranging from marshes to willow thickets to hayfields. In fact, Red-winged Blackbirds are one of the most likely birds to be seen along highways.

Males are first to return to breeding areas in spring, usually soon after ice has left the marshes that they favor. Those that are older and more experienced claim territories that are larger or have the greatest potential for nest sites and insect prey. Females arrive about a week later and, if a male has garnered an especially rich territory, up to eight may subdivide it and mate with him. Here they raise their young, typically with little help from the male, other than his defense of the nest from predators and other Red-winged Blackbirds.

Nests are composed of leaves and stems woven into upright vegetation such as cattails. They lay three to four eggs which are greenish-blue and scrawled with blacks and browns. The eggs hatch in 11 to 13 days and the stubby-tailed young flutter weakly from the nest 12 days later. A second clutch of eggs often utilizes the same nest.

Red-winged Blackbirds form immense flocks during the non-nesting season. An estimated total of 20 million individuals was recorded on a Christmas Bird Count at the Squaw Creek National Wildlife Refuge in Missouri in 1978. This accounted for about one-third of all of the Red-winged Blackbirds counted on Christmas Bird Counts that year, demonstrating how amassed they sometimes become.

EASTERN MEADOWLARK
▶ common in fields and on fences
▶ black V on bright yellow breast
▶ white outer feathers on short, wide tail show when bird is flushed
▶ several rapid wingbeats alternate with short glides

WESTERN MEADOWLARK
▶ nearly identical to Eastern but paler above, and the yellow throat extends a bit further onto the cheek

EASTERN MEADOWLARK

Sturnella magna

WESTERN MEADOWLARK

Sturnella neglecta

There is no bird so familiar throughout the farmlands of America's Midwest as the meadowlark. Nor is there a more faithful harbinger of spring. The first song of the year at the icy break of a March morning while patches of snow are still on the ground reassures farmers that spring fieldwork can soon get underway. Singing meadowlarks perch on fence posts, utility wires, or slight rises on the ground, displaying their bright yellow breasts with the overlying black bibs. When in flight, they show the white outer feathers of their short tails. They are stocky birds, and about nine-inches in length. Due to their shape, short wings, and rapid wing beat, they resemble small quail.

America's two meadowlark species are named for the regions of the country they occupy. Eastern Meadowlarks range from the East Coast west to mid-Kansas and central Minnesota. Western Meadowlarks breed northwest of a line extending from northern Michigan through northern Illinois, southern Iowa, northwestern Missouri to southeastern Kansas. Therefore, both species live together through a broad swath of the Great Plains. Though nearly identical in appearance, they are readily distinguished by sound. The Western Meadowlark's song is bubbling and melodious as compared to the Eastern Meadolark's simple, plaintive whistle.

Meadowlarks winter well north into the Midwest, facilitating their early arrival at breeding areas. They choose hayfields, pastures, and road ditches, building grass cup nests directly on the ground and shielding them with a roof of bent-over grasses. The three to six eggs are white with dark speckles. They hatch in two weeks. The young leave the nest by 12 days of age, before being able to fly well. Meadowlarks eat insects, such as grasshoppers. Wintering birds join together in small flocks and subsist on weed seeds and waste grains.

The Western Meadowlark's delightful song is likely the reason it was selected as the State Bird of Kansas, Nebraska, North Dakota, Wyoming, Montana, and Oregon.

Western Meadowlark   Eastern Meadowlark

IDENTIFICATION TIPS
► large, iridescent; larger than a Robin
► long wedge-shaped tail is broader at the end
► male has iridescent purple-green-blue on head,
  and a deep bronze or dull purple back
► flocks with cowbirds, Red-winged Blackbirds,
  and starlings

COMMON GRACKLE
Quiscalus quiscula

These gleaming blackbirds with the long, keel-shaped tails are familiar to urban and rural residents alike. They are conspicuous in yards, parks, and along shores as they waddle about, searching the ground for such delicacies as worms, bugs, and bits of vegetation. Most people know them, but not by their official name, instead referring to them only as blackbirds.

Highly social, Common Grackles usually nest, travel, and forage in groups. Flock members sometimes threaten each other with the ritualized behavior of pointing their bills skyward. Or, they simply announce their presence with their familiar screeching squawk, delivered energetically with the simultaneous flaring of the wings and tail. When alarmed or to keep contact with each other while flying about, they repeatedly emit *chack* calls. Seemingly intelligent, they learn by observation such behaviors as dipping food items into bird baths to soften them.

Common Grackles are one of spring's early arrivers and breeders. Up to 30 pairs will nest together in pine groves or dense foliage lining roads, streams, and lakes. Females, which are less glossy and slightly smaller than the 12-inch males, incubate the three to six pale green, brown-blotched eggs. The eggs hatch in about 13 days. Rearing requires another 12 to 15 days. Although silent around nesting colonies, the traffic of the busy parents can become so constant as to be noticed, especially during the latter part of the nesting period. Repeated flights into the trees bring food deliveries for the hungry young, while on outbound flights the parents carry small, white objects in their bills. These are fecal sacks that nestling songbirds commonly produce. They are dropped at a distance, presumably to lessen detection of the nests by predators. Common Grackles nest only once each year.

These well-known blackbirds breed from the East Coast west to the Rocky Mountains and well north into Canada. Following the nesting season, they gather into larger flocks, often with other kinds of blackbirds. The majority winter in the southern states.

IDENTIFICATION TIPS
▶ small blackbirds; male is black with a brown head
▶ female is all gray with a short, finch-like bill
▶ often in mixed flocks with Red-winged Blackbirds
or Common Grackles
▶ when with other blackbirds, Cowbirds are smaller
and feed on the ground with their tails lifted high

BROWN-HEADED COWBIRD

Molothrus ater

These six-and-a-half inch birds live throughout most of North America in habitats ranging from forests to fields to towns and cities. Although traditionally in the company of cattle, there is hardly anywhere that one does not hear their squeaks and liquid gurgles or see a small band of the black, brown-headed males tilting and bill-raising to each other on an overhead perch. Or, three to four might be seen flying rapidly in a tight group low over the ground in pursuit of a single female. Cowbirds are easy to see, not only because they are common but because they tend to perch in the open. The drab, mouse-gray females especially use open perches to better observe potential hosts for their eggs when nearing egg-laying time. Egg laying can occur from March through August.

Most people are annoyed to learn that Brown-headed Cowbirds escape parental duties by fostering their young out to other birds. They are further disturbed to learn that the foster parents usually sacrifice their own young while unwittingly raising baby cowbirds. Brown-headed Cowbirds apparently evolved this remarkable behavior when following bison herds to feed on the associated insects and debris, thus abandoning the eggs that they had laid. Those eggs placed in the nests of other birds were sometimes raised and those cowbirds passed on refinements that caused the strategy to become even more successful. These included light-colored, speckled eggs that match those of many other birds, and smallish eggs to trick smallish birds. Brown-headed Cowbirds also produce more total eggs during the season so that they are able to parasitize a number of nests and thereby "hedge their bets." These eggs have a comparatively short incubation period so that they are likely to hatch sooner than the host's eggs. Also, Brown-headed Cowbirds tend to deposit their egg before the host's clutch is complete.

Over 120 bird species are known to have been parasitized by Brown-headed Cowbirds, including the Chipping Sparrow shown here. Chipping Sparrows are examples of birds that occasionally raise one or two of their own nestlings in addition to the Brown-headed Cowbird chick.

IDENTIFICATION TIPS
► adult male has solid black head and black "T" on the tail
► female has orange-yellow belly and streaked, olive-brown back
► 2 white wing bars

♂

♀

BALTIMORE ORIOLE

Icterus galbula

These seven-inch members of the Blackbird Family are among the most popular of birds. The dazzling males are known best. Females are subtly-colored and can be confused with other species unless one recognizes their similarity to males in shape, behavior, and habitat. Both sexes sing but it is the male's assortment of clear, flute-like whistles that especially attracts our attention. Both sexes emit a low chatter when disturbed.

Baltimore Orioles breed from the Midwest to the East Coast where early settlers named them for Lord Baltimore, whose family colonized Maryland. The bright, orange and black feathers matched his family colors. Throughout the Baltimore Oriole's range, they favor tall trees along streams and in suburban yards. Because they glean insects from foliage, they wait until leaf-out before returning to their breeding range, typically in late April. It is then that they begin courting and are most vocal.

These spectacular songbirds are perhaps best known for their hanging nests which are so intricate as to require up to a week of construction. Woven of grasses, strips of bark, stems, hair, and other fibers, nests are usually positioned high on the hanging tips of outer branches and so well hidden among leaves as to not be detected until after leaf fall. Sometimes several nests will be found within a few nearby trees. Some people delight in hanging out pieces of colored string that they later see woven into the nests.

A single clutch of four to five splotched eggs (pale gray to blue-white marked with dark colors) is produced each year. Incubation and the rearing of young requires about a month. Summering Baltimore Orioles will occasionally take "nectar" from hummingbird feeders and specially designed Oriole feeders. People can also attract them by putting out cut-up citrus and jelly.

Baltimore Orioles fall quiet during the heart of the nesting period. Like many other songbirds, they begin to sing again just before their departure in August. Over half of the year is spent on the wintering range which includes primarily Central America and Mexico, though some winter in the extreme southern United States.

Fittingly, the Baltimore Oriole is the State Bird of Maryland.

PURPLE FINCH IDENTIFICATION TIPS

▶ sparrow sized; male is dull cranberry red and is more uniformly colored than other red finches

▶ female and immature are heavily striped; differentiated from sparrows by their heavier beaks, deeper tail notches, and undulating flight; differentiated from house finches by the broad dark jaw stripe, broad light stripe behind the eye, and larger beak

Purple Finch
♀

Purple Finch
♂

House Finch
♂

House Finch
♀

HOUSE FINCH IDENTIFICATION TIPS

▶ smaller than Purple Finch

▶ male is brighter red than male Purple Finch, and red is more restricted to the head and back; also dark stripes on the sides and belly

▶ striped female is told from the female Purple Finch by its smaller bill and plain face (no eye stripe or dark mustache)

PURPLE FINCH

Carpodacus purpureus

HOUSE FINCH

Carpodacus mexicanus

These two closely-related finches are easily confused, both being about five inches in length and having reddish-colored males and brownish females. There are opportunities to compare them, however, when they are together at winter bird feeders. The Male Purple Finch's red is slightly lavender, whereas the House Finch's is a shade towards orange. Purple Finch males may have faint streaking on their flanks, while House Finch males have brown streaking along their sides. Female Purple Finches are boldly streaked with a definite light streak behind the eye, whereas House Finches are finely streaked with brown throughout. Finally, the Purple Finch's tail-tip is notched, while the House Finch's is square.

Throughout most of the Midwest, the best way to separate the two finches is to let them separate themselves. Purple Finches migrate in May to nest in coniferous forests of the northern Great Lakes States and Canada, whereas House Finches remain within their winter range. Male House Finches mark the onset of the March nesting season with sweet warbling songs. Nests are made of fine grasses in such places as spruce trees, hanging flower pots, and decorative wreaths, where protected from wind and rain. They lay four to five pale blue, dark speckled eggs. The eggs hatch in two weeks and the young fledge two weeks later. House Finches nest two to three times a season, building a new nest each time.

Purple Finches usually nest in conifers within their northern range. Their eggs, incubation, and rearing periods are similar to the House Finch's. They return to winter with us in October. Their abundance from year to year varies greatly.

Previous to the 1940s, House Finches were known only west of the Rocky Mountains. Because of their beautiful color and song, some were captured and sold in the east as caged pets under the name "Hollywood Finches." Some were released or escaped on Long Island, New York, in 1940. Within ten years, they began to extend their range westward from there, in what was one of the most explosive range expansions ever documented. They had reached Ohio by 1972 and were first nesting in Missouri in1983. Currently, they range westward to central Kansas and Nebraska, meeting their original western range.

Purple Finch   House Finch

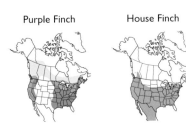

IDENTIFICATION TIPS

▶ bright yellow summer male is unmistakable; contrasting black wings, tail, and forehead patch

▶ winter males, females, and immature birds have unstreaked backs and breasts (olive-yellow colored, darker back), and blackish wings with conspicuous wing bars

▶ notched tail

▶ stubby finch bill

▶ whitish rump

▶ deeply undulating flight

AMERICAN GOLDFINCH
Carduelis tristis

These brilliant, four-and-a-half inch finches are common, especially in the countryside, across the North American continent. They especially associate with weedy fields over which they can be recognized by the repeated twittering that accompanies their looping, roller-coaster flight. If one is seen, there is usually at least one more, dipping and rising against the sky.

Sometimes called "wild canaries," males in breeding plumage are vivid yellow, contrasting with black wings and tails. Females are a muted yellowish-tan in place of the male's yellow as are winter-plumaged males. It is the duller-plumaged individuals that are most commonly seen because most people know them best in winter when flocks visit bird feeders. By mid-spring, soon after the males have begun to brighten, they move to the country. Flocks may periodically re-invade towns, such as when dandelions go to seed, but most are afield from May through September.

American Goldfinches initiate nesting later in summer than any other North American bird. They pair off in spring, but most wait until July to build nests in synchrony with the ripening of thistle flowers. Thistle down is used to construct nests, while partially-digested thistle seeds are fed to young. Nesting habitat includes shrubby field borders and road ditches. Nests are typically situated within a few feet of the ground where a crotch is formed by four upright branches. The nests are only three inches across and so compactly constructed that they are reported to hold water. The miniature eggs are light-colored (bluish-white) and number four to six. The female builds the nest and incubates her eggs for the required two weeks. Both parents feed the nestlings for 12 to 14 days until fledging and for an additional three weeks following their departure from the nest.

The American Goldfinch is the State Bird of Iowa and Washington.

HOUSE SPARROW

Passer domesticus

These busy, five-inch birds are especially populous in cities, towns, and on farms. The male is recognized by his black bib, whereas the female is one of the plainest of birds. House Sparrows can become monotonous because of their commonness and their incessant chirping. They feed and nest in flocks and are most disliked for their habit of stuffing their grass and debris nests in the nooks and crannies of buildings.

House Sparrows are related to the weaver finches of Africa, a family that constructs bulky, woven nests of grass in trees. On the rare occasions that House Sparrow nests are built in trees, they somewhat resemble those of their relatives in being spherical with side entrances. The House Sparrow's four to six eggs are bluish and speckled with brown. They are commonly cushioned on a bed of feathers that the female has collected from the vicinity. The eggs hatch in 11 days and the young fly from the nest two weeks later. House Sparrows are nonmigratory, and they nest repeatedly from March through August.

Also known as "English Sparrows," House Sparrows are native to the Old World. Their origin in this country can be traced to introductions in Brooklyn, New York, and elsewhere in the early 1850s. Their subsequent expansion westward across North America was facilitated by the establishment of farms and towns. They reached the Mississippi River by 1870 and by 1900, they ranged from the East to the West Coast.

It is thought that they similarly advanced westward through Europe with the advent of civilization between 7000 and 1000 BC. The domestication of livestock is believed responsible, as the little birds feed on the insects associated with horse manure. This relationship may explain why they were in greatest numbers in the United States around 1900, when horse use was very common.

In England, they have been mysteriously disappearing from many cities and farms during recent decades. In America, however, they remain fairly abundant because of their use of human structures for nesting, and because of their diverse food habits. They forage around fast food restaurants and picnic areas, and even glean insects from car grills in parking lots. Their association with humans has given them a "leg up" on native birds, such as bluebirds, with whom they sometimes compete for nesting sites.

INDEX